# Smart Choices

# Smart Choices

*A Practical Guide to*
*Making Better Life Decisions*

John S. Hammond
Ralph L. Keeney
Howard Raiffa

**Broadway Books**
*New York*

Parts of Chapters 5 and 6 were previously published as "Even Swaps: A Rational Method for Making Trade-offs" in *Harvard Business Review* (March–April 1998). Parts of Chapter 10 were previously published as "The Hidden Traps in Decision Making" in *Harvard Business Review* (September–October 1998).

PRINTED IN THE UNITED STATES OF AMERICA

First Broadway Books trade paperback edition published 2002

Library of Congress Cataloging-in-Publication Data

Hammond, John S., 1937–
Smart choices: a practical guide to making better life decisions / John S. Hammond, Ralph L. Keeney, Howard Raiffa.
p.   cm.
Originally published: Boston, Mass.: Harvard Business School Press, c1999.
Includes bibliographical references and index.
1. Decision making.   I. Keeney, Ralph L., 1944–   II. Raiffa, Howard, 1924–
III. Title.
BF448 .H35 2002
153.8'3—dc21                                        2001043463

ISBN 0-7679-0886-4

10   9   8   7   6   5   4   3

# Contents

# Introduction to the Paperback Edition

Readers have spoken. They made *Smart Choices* a bestseller in hardback, indicating that they consider decision making a critical life skill.

*Smart Choices* garnered numerous positive reviews from readers and professionals alike. It was selected for the Book of the Year award by the prestigious CPR Institute for Dispute Resolution, and it has been translated into over a dozen languages. Of course, this response has been very gratifying to us.

But the real value of *Smart Choices* is how it has helped people make better decisions. Life is about choices, about priorities, and one of the biggest ways that you can influence the quality of your life is by improving the quality of your decisions. It's not only about the "big stuff," but about the little things, too, which can overwhelm you if you aren't equipped with the right decision-making tools. As a result of reading our book, many people are navigating their lives more successfully and feeling more confident about taking action.

The success of *Smart Choices* has also led to opportunities to give lectures and seminars on decision making. Afterward, we are asked a variety of questions by people who haven't yet read our book and learned the simple system for making a smart choice. Since these may be your questions as well, here are our answers:

- **What does this book offer me?**    *Smart Choices* is a systematic way of thinking about your decisions—whether they could change your life or simply your day. This book presents a process to help you make better choices in your personal life and at work. The process teaches you how to focus on what is really important and guides you to the "right decision." This not only reduces the stress and anxiety that you feel when facing difficult choices, but increases your confidence in your decision and better enables you to explain your choice to others.

- **What kinds of decisions does the book address?**    *Any* decision worthy of serious thought, whether it requires two minutes or two months. For example, workplace decisions such as whether to enter into a new activity or which employee to hire or how to arrange a travel itinerary. Personal decisions such as which new house to buy and what price to offer or whom to invite to a dinner party.

- **Do the ideas in *Smart Choices* really work?**    Readers say, "Yes!" We have heard from many, many people who have successfully applied the ideas to important decisions in their lives. They have told us that *Smart Choices* helped them decide on career moves, home and car purchases, whether to marry or get divorced, which college to attend, where to vacation, work issues, as well as many other types of choices.

- **Will I understand the ideas in this book?**    Not only will you understand them, but according to readers, you'll really enjoy them. The presenter of the book award called it "ingenious in its simplicity," and understandable "even for insomniacs at four in the morning." In making some types of decisions, numbers are helpful. It's simply more useful to know that a prospective house costs $149,000 than to know that it is "moderately priced." If you recognize that a 20 percent down payment on this house is about $30,000, you will have no difficulty with the arithmetic in this book.

- **Has *Smart Choices* been used in the classroom?**    *Smart Choices* is widely used in classrooms. Professors worldwide are using it as core material in decision-making courses in diverse fields ranging from business to psychology to public policy to nursing, to name just a few. We are thrilled about this for two reasons. First, this has happened in spite of the fact that we didn't write *Smart Choices* to be a text. Perhaps that's the very reason for its success in the classroom: it's easily readable yet rigorous. Second, seeing decision making taught in so many fields affirms our core belief that it is fundamental to *all* fields. We would love to see more courses about this life skill taught to undergraduates and high school students, too.

- **Is it used in executive and professional training programs?** Once again, yes. Good decision-making skills are fundamental to all occupations and to the success of any organization.

- **What about giving it to friends and associates?**    According to all reports, it makes a wonderful gift. We've heard countless stories of people who have given it to many on their holiday giving list, to college or high school students at graduation, to a friend or family member who is making a tough decision, or to a colleague at work. Everyone will be much better off by making better decisions more easily.

We hope that you enjoy *Smart Choices* and reap its benefits in all aspects of your life. We also would be delighted to hear about your experiences. (Contacts: Hammond: jhammond@DBA1968.hbs. edu; Keeney: RKeeney@marshall.usc.edu; Raiffa; hraiffa@hbs.edu)

John S. Hammond
Ralph L. Keeney
Howard Raiffa

# Preface

You're stuck. You're in a quandary. You face an important decision, and you're not sure what to do.

You've come to the right book.

You know your success depends on making smart choices, so you want to know how to become a better decision maker.

You, too, have come to the right book.

We wrote *Smart Choices* to bridge the gap between how people actually *do* make decisions and what researchers—including the three of us—have discovered over the last 50 years about how they *should* make decisions. We have distilled for you the essence of decision-making research, combined it with experience and common sense, and presented it in a straightforward, accessible form for your regular use. The result should be hundreds, maybe thousands, of better decisions that will help you reach your goals, reduce wasted time and money, and avoid hassle, worry, and regret—in short, a higher quality of life through improved decision making.

The arguments for acquiring superb decision-making skills are compelling. You spend a significant portion of your time and psychic energy making choices. Who you are, what you are, where you are, how successful you are, how happy you are all derive in large part from your decisions. In short, the decisions you make, make *you*. Yet decision making is seldom taught as a skill in its own right. Considering its importance, one would expect that high schools, colleges, and graduate schools would routinely offer courses in decision making and that dozens of good books on the topic would be available. Sadly, neither is true. There are few courses, few books.

## *Smart Choices* Provides a Roadmap for Good Decisions

In these pages, we present a clear process and a set of user-friendly techniques for making smart choices. We show you what you need to consider in evaluating your options and the steps you need to take to arrive at the smart choice. The essence of our approach is *divide and conquer:* break your decision into its key elements; identify those most relevant to your decision; apply some hard, systematic thinking; and make your decision. Our approach is *proactive,* encouraging you to seek out decision-making opportunities rather than wait for problems to present themselves.

*Smart Choices* is a distillation of all we have learned from our more than 100 collective years of teaching and writing about decision making, as well as the practical experience we have gained in consulting on thousands of important decisions facing individuals, families, businesses, nonprofits, and governments.

You can apply our method to any decision worthy of serious thought. It will help you make smart personal decisions—from which new house to purchase, to which mutual fund to buy, to whether to have elective surgery. And it will help you make smart work decisions—from which job candidate to hire, to which business strategy to pursue, to which travel itinerary to book.

## *Smart Choices* **Is Clear and Easy to Understand**

One reason that few people have been able to benefit from all the existing research on decision making is that the insights are expressed in academic, technical prose. We strip away the jargon, allowing you to grasp the essence of the ideas quickly and surely. For your most complicated and important decisions, we provide step-by-step procedures that will help you grapple with tough tradeoffs, clarify uncertainties, evaluate risks, and make a series of linked decisions in the right sequence.

After you've applied our method to a few of your decisions, you'll find yourself growing more and more comfortable with the process and techniques. You'll become less intimidated by making decisions, and you'll start making them faster and more easily, with less frustration and, most important, with better results.

As you hone your decision-making skills, drawing on the lessons in this book, we are confident that your life will change for the better.

Once you have read the book, you'll find that the Roadmap to Smart Choices is a complete summary of the contents. Since it mirrors the chapters, it also serves as a quick reference to any part of the book and as a refresher for its concepts. The Roadmap is at the end of the book in place of an index.

The hardest part about writing a book is getting the words right. Fortunately, we had outstanding help. We are grateful for the astute guidance from Nikki Sabin, our HBS Press editor, for the excellent editing by Susan Boulanger and Nick Carr, for the tireless word-processing and advice from Nancy Orth, and for the helpful suggestions of many who commented on our earlier manuscripts.

John S. Hammond
Ralph L. Keeney
Howard Raiffa

# CHAPTER 1

# Making Smart Choices

OUR DECISIONS SHAPE OUR LIVES. Made consciously or unconsciously, with good or bad consequences, they represent the fundamental tool we use in facing the opportunities, the challenges, and the uncertainties of life.

- Should I go to college? If so, where? To study what?
- What career should I pursue? What job should I take?
- Should I get married now, or wait? Should I have children? If so, when and how many?
- Where should I live? Should I trade up to a larger house? What can I contribute to my community?
- Which job candidate should I hire? What marketing strategy should I recommend for my company?
- Since I feel unfulfilled, should I change jobs? Go back to school? Move?
- How should I invest my savings? When should I retire? To do what? Where?

Such questions mark the progress of our lives and our careers, and the way we answer them determines, to a large extent, our place in society and in the world. Our success in all the roles we play—student, worker, boss, citizen, spouse, parent, individual—turns on the decisions we make.

## Making Decisions Is a Fundamental Life Skill

Some decisions will be fairly obvious—"no-brainers." Your bank account is low, but you have a two-week vacation coming up and you want to get away to someplace warm to relax with your family. Will you accept your in-laws' offer of free use of their Florida beachfront condo? Sure. You like your employer and feel ready to move forward in your career. Will you step in for your boss for three weeks while she attends a professional development course? Of course.

But the no-brainers are the exceptions. Most of the important decisions you'll face in life are tough and complex, with no easy or obvious solutions. And they probably won't affect you alone. They'll affect your family, your friends, your coworkers, and many others known and unknown. Making good decisions is thus one of the most important determinants of how well you meet your responsibilities and achieve your personal and professional goals. In short, *the ability to make smart choices is a fundamental life skill.*

Most of us, however, dread making hard decisions. By definition, tough choices have high stakes and serious consequences; they involve numerous and complex considerations; and they expose us to the judgments of others. The need to make a difficult decision puts us at risk of anxiety, confusion, doubt, error, regret, embarrassment, loss. No wonder we find it hard to settle down and choose. In living through a major decision, we suffer periods of alternating self-doubt and overconfidence, of procrastination, of wheel-spinning and flip-flopping, of frustration, even of desperation. Our discomfort often leads us to make decisions too quickly, or too slowly, or too arbitrarily. We flip a coin, toss a dart, let someone else—or time—decide. The result: a mediocre choice, dependent on luck for success. It's only afterwards that we realize we could have made a smarter choice. And by then it's too late.

## You *Can* Learn to Make Better Decisions

Why do we have such trouble? It's simple: *we don't know how to make decisions well.* Despite the importance of decision making to our lives, few of us ever receive any training in it. So we are left to learn from experience. But experience is a costly, inefficient teacher that teaches us bad habits along with good ones. Because decision situations vary so markedly, the experience of making one important decision often seems of little use when facing the next. How is deciding what job to take or what house to buy similar to deciding what school to send your children to, what medical treatment to pursue for a serious illness, or what balance to strike among cost, aesthetics, and function in planning a new office park?

The connection among the decisions you make lies not in *what* you're deciding, but in *how* you decide. The only way to really raise your odds of making a good decision is to learn to use a good decision-making process—one that gets you to the best solution with a minimal loss of time, energy, money, and composure.

An effective decision-making process fulfills these six criteria:

- It focuses on what's important.
- It is logical and consistent.
- It acknowledges both subjective and objective factors and blends analytical with intuitive thinking.
- It requires only as much information and analysis as is necessary to resolve a particular dilemma.
- It encourages and guides the gathering of relevant information and informed opinion.
- It is straightforward, reliable, easy to use, and flexible.

A decision-making approach that addresses these criteria can be practiced on decisions major and minor—what movie to see, what car to buy, what vacation to take, what investment to make, what department head to hire, what medical treatment to pursue. And the more you use such an approach, the more efficient and effective it will become. As you grow more skilled and your confidence grows, making decisions will become second nature to you. In fact, you may find your friends and associates asking you for help and advice with their tough choices!

## Use the PrOACT Approach to Make Smart Choices

This book provides you with a straightforward, proven approach for making decisions. It does not tell you *what* to decide, but it does show you *how.* Our approach meets the six criteria listed above. It helps you to see both the tangible and the intangible aspects of your decision situation more clearly and to translate all pertinent facts, feelings, opinions, beliefs, and advice into the best possible choice. Highly flexible, it is applicable to business and professional decisions, to personal decisions, to family decisions—to any decision you need to make.

One thing the method won't do is make hard decisions easy. That's impossible. Hard decisions are hard because they're complex, and no one can make that complexity disappear. But you can manage complexity sensibly. How? Just like you'd climb a mountain: one step at a time.

Our approach takes one step at a time. We have found that even the most complex decision can be analyzed and resolved by considering a set of eight elements (see below). The first five—**Pr**oblem, **O**bjectives, **A**lternatives, **C**onsequences, and **T**radeoffs—constitute the core of our approach and are applicable to virtually any decision. The acronym for these—PrOACT—serves as a reminder that the best approach to decision situations is a *proactive* one. The worst thing you can do is wait until a decision is forced on you—or made for you.

## The Eight Elements of Smart Choices

| |
|---|
| **Pr**oblem |
| **O**bjectives |
| **A**lternatives |
| **C**onsequences |
| **T**radeoffs |
| Uncertainty |
| Risk Tolerance |
| Linked Decisions |

The three remaining elements—uncertainty, risk tolerance, and linked decisions—help clarify decisions in volatile or evolving environments. Some decisions won't involve these elements, but many of your most important decisions will.

The essence of the PrOACT approach is to divide and conquer. To resolve a complex decision situation, you break it into these elements and think systematically about each one, focusing on those that are key to your particular situation. Then you reassemble your thoughts and analysis into the smart choice. So, although our method may not make a hard decision *easy,* it will certainly make it *easier.*

## There Are Eight Keys to Effective Decision Making

Let's take a brief look at each of the elements of the PrOACT approach to see how they work and how they fit together.

**Work on the right decision problem.**   What must you decide? Is it which health club to join? Or whether to join one at all as opposed to walking more or buying some home gym equipment? Is it who to hire to manage your company's information systems department? Or whether you should even have an information systems department as opposed to outsourcing the function to an outside provider? The way you frame your decision at the outset can make all the difference. To choose well, you need to state your decision problems carefully, acknowledging their complexity and avoiding unwarranted assumptions and option-limiting prejudices.

**Specify your objectives.**   Your decision should get you where you want to go. If you have to hire a new employee, do you want someone who's a disciplined team player or a creative free spirit? Do you want a fresh perspective or solid experience? A decision is a means to an end. Ask yourself what you most want to accomplish and which of your interests, values, concerns, fears, and aspirations are most relevant to achieving your goal. Thinking through your objectives will give direction to your decision making.

**Create imaginative alternatives.**   Your alternatives represent the different courses of action you have to choose from. Should you take sides in a family argument or stand aside from the rising tide of accusation and acrimony? Or should you seek a resolution palatable to everyone concerned? If you didn't have different alternatives, you wouldn't be facing a decision. But have you considered *all* the alternatives or at least a wide range of creative and desirable ones? Remember: your decision can be no better than your best alternative.

**Understand the consequences.**   How well do your alternatives satisfy your objectives? Alternatives beckon and beguile, but beyond them lie sometimes sobering, sometimes exciting consequences. Abandoning the corporate treadmill for your own sailboat chartering outfit in Aruba may sound enticing, but what would be the consequences for your spouse's career, your school-age children, your aging parents, your cancer-prone skin? Assessing frankly the consequences of each alternative will help you to identify those that best meet your objectives—*all* your objectives.

**Grapple with your tradeoffs.**   Because objectives frequently con-
flict with one another, you'll need to strike a balance. Some of *this*
must sometimes be sacrificed in favor of some of *that*. Your career
is important to you, but so is your family. You may decide, therefore, to reduce your business travel or even to cut back on your
hours at the office. You'll lose some career momentum and possibly some income, but you'll gain time with your spouse and your
kids. In most complex decisions, there is no one perfect alternative. Different alternatives fulfill different constellations of
objectives. Your task is to choose intelligently among the less-
than-perfect possibilities. To do so, you need to set priorities by
openly addressing the need for tradeoffs among competing objectives.

**Clarify your uncertainties.**   What could happen in the future,
and how likely is it that it will? To decide how much money to set
aside for your daughter's college education fund, you must assess
a number of uncertainties. Will she apply to an Ivy League university or a state college? Will she be accepted? Are her academic,
artistic, or athletic skills likely to earn her a scholarship? Will she
want to work while studying? Will she need a car? Uncertainty
makes choosing far more difficult. But effective decision making
demands that you confront uncertainty, judging the likelihood of
different outcomes and assessing their possible impacts.

**Think hard about your risk tolerance.**   When decisions involve
uncertainties, the desired consequence may not be the one that
actually results. A much-deliberated bone marrow transplant
may or may not halt cancer. A low-risk investment in municipal

bonds could result in major financial losses. People vary in their tolerance of such risks and, depending on the stakes involved, in the risk they will accept from one decision to the next. A conscious awareness of your willingness to accept risk will make your decision-making process smoother and more effective. It will help you to choose an alternative with the right level of risk *for you.*

**Consider linked decisions.**   What you decide today could influence your choices tomorrow, and your goals for tomorrow should influence your choices today. Thus many important decisions are linked over time. A highway commissioner may decide to buy land now to create options for accommodating possible increases in traffic in the future. He thus circumvents potential jumps in land values or increases in community resistance which could foreclose future options. The key to dealing effectively with linked decisions is to isolate and resolve near-term issues while gathering the information needed to resolve those that will arise later. By sequencing your actions to fully exploit what you learn along the way, you will be doing your best, despite an uncertain world, to make smarter choices.

The eight PrOACT elements provide a framework that can profoundly redirect your decision making, enriching your possibilities and increasing your chances of finding a satisfying solution. Before discussing each element in the coming chapters, we'll begin here with a brief and somewhat simplified case study that shows the PrOACT process at work.

## APPLICATION

## To Sell a Business or Not?

Many years ago, an acquaintance of ours who we'll call Bill established a soundproofing business in Brooklyn, New York, with his friend Stan. It had the usual rocky start faced by most new businesses—getting it established required a lot of hard work—but after 20 tough years Bill and his partner were at last happy with where their company stood. It had grown; it was successful; and their key employees were skilled, loyal, and reliable. The unremitting stresses and strains of owning a small business had eased.

Bill, an active and restless man who liked challenge and change, now worried about becoming complacent and losing his edge. Taking a proactive look at his situation, he began to evaluate his needs and concluded that he wanted to sell his half of the company. He thought he might go on to launch a new business of some kind. He shared his thoughts with Stan, and Stan indicated a willingness to buy Bill out.

Then Bill started thinking about how to price his share of the business. He knew that the company was worth $1,300,000, giving his half a value of $650,000. But he felt that was much more than Stan could afford. He decided, tentatively, to set the price at $400,000. When he talked over his intentions with his wife, Marie, and their three grown children, however, they expressed considerable discomfort with the course he was considering. They remembered vividly, even if Bill himself didn't, the grueling toll taken by the long hours and high stress of the early years spent establishing and building the company. Was he really ready to go through that again at age 57? And if he did sell, shouldn't he get the full rewards of his labor—shouldn't Stan have to pay the real price? As Bill listened to their arguments, he realized that he, too, was uncomfortable with the decision he was about to make. He sought our advice.

Our first priority was to help Bill formulate his decision *problem* clearly. Why sell? He was bored; he wanted a change. He planned, somewhat vaguely, to develop another business, location and type undecided. He also planned, again vaguely, to look into moving to the West Coast—the climate appealed to him, and he and Marie would have more opportunities to golf, sail, fish, ski, and pursue the other outdoor activities they loved.

Bill needed to give direction to his decision problem by assessing his *objectives* explicitly. How much did he really want the invigoration of a new physical environment and way of life? the intellectual challenge of gaining expertise in a new area? the mental and emotional effort of building a business from the ground up? With more focus and thought, Bill defined his primary objectives: participating in outdoor recreational activities, being challenged intellectually, and minimizing stress. He clearly valued loyalty to his partner as well, because he was willing to sacrifice to him a significant portion of his business equity.

We began next to look at *alternatives.* Bill had ruled out the status quo, but he had considered only one other option: selling out to his partner for $400,000. But even given his determination to sell, a higher price would better enable him to fulfill his objectives—he shouldn't overlook that alternative. In addition, we helped Bill develop some other, more creative choices. He could get $650,000 by finding a buyer other than his partner. Or his partner could pay $400,000 immediately and $250,000 in installments over time. Or Bill and Stan could both sell, with Stan, if he wished, remaining to manage the business under the new ownership.

Bill's new insight into his objectives led him to reflect more deeply on the *consequences* of this expanded, but still-limited range of alternatives. Had he considered the bite that capital gains taxes would take out of his investment capital? Would the remaining sum give him the flexibility to start over while maintaining the degree of leisure and comfort that he and Marie had come to enjoy? The financial picture for a sellout, given the tax situation, didn't look as·attractive as it once had.

We pressed Bill to consider the *tradeoffs* between his own financial well-being and his loyalty to his partner. We asked if, magically, his partner were somehow to come up with $650,000 to buy the business, would Bill turn around and write his partner a check for $250,000? He responded, naturally, with a resounding "No!"

We also helped Bill think through the other tradeoffs inherent in his objectives. He wanted to enjoy outdoor life in a milder climate, but he wasn't ready to retire. On the other hand, he didn't want to go back to spending all his time working or worrying about work, either. He already had one grandchild, with another on the way, and he wanted to spend more time with them than he had been able to spend with their parents. Clearly, starting over with a new business would require significant personal sacrifices, not to mention the considerable *risks* and *uncertainties* of launching a new venture in a new market in a new place. Bill wasn't afraid of uncertainty and risk—he was a businessman, after all—but this time around he wouldn't be able to rely on Stan's expertise and support. After an association of more than 20 years, he had come to value Stan's perspective highly.

Armed with a full and fresh view of his decision problem, Bill thought further about the issues we had explored. He discussed his objectives and alternatives with his family and his partner. Bill's ultimate *smart choice,* a complete reversal of his original plan, was not to sell out. Instead, he and his wife moved to southern California, where he established a West Coast branch of the soundproofing business. They enjoyed their new lifestyle, and Bill found it invigorating to build a new business almost—but not quite—from scratch. He did so well with the business, in fact, that when, eight years later, he was really ready to retire, his partner bought him out for $1.7 million.

## Start Making Your Own Smart Choices Now

Bill's experience illustrates the benefits of learning *how* to make good decisions. Of course, a good decision doesn't necessarily guarantee a good result, just as a bad decision doesn't necessarily guarantee a bad result. The careless can hit it lucky; the careful can be shot down. But a good decision does increase the odds of success and at the same time satisfies our very human desire to control the forces that affect our lives. In the chapters that follow, we will lay out, step by step, the PrOACT approach for decision making—the method that proved so valuable to Bill. Reading these chapters will enable you to improve the way you make the decisions that determine the course of your own life.

Before we plunge in, though, we want to review a couple of important tips that will help ensure that you get the full benefits of our approach.

First and foremost, always focus your thinking where it matters most. Cycle quickly through the eight elements to gain a broad perspective on your decision problem. Typically, for all but the most complex decisions, you will not need to consider all the elements in depth. Usually, only one or two elements will emerge as the most critical for the decision at hand.

Sometimes, the simple act of setting out your problem, objectives, alternatives, consequences, and tradeoffs, as well as any uncertainties, risks, or linked decision factors, will fully clarify the decision, pointing the way to the smart choice. If not, you should try reconfiguring your problem in various ways. Display it graphically, as a table, diagram, or chart, for example. Restate it in several forms, using different words, phrasings, and emphasis. Describe your problem to others, asking for their opinions and advice. For Bill, imagining himself giving his partner $250,000 in cash was an eye-opener, as were his family's recollections about the struggles and stresses of the past.

Although the systematic approach we prescribe will greatly increase the chances of reaching a smart choice—as it did with Bill—it doesn't assure it. You must also avoid certain psychological traps that can derail your thinking. Psychologists have shown, for example, that the first ideas that come into our head when we start out to make a decision can have an undue impact on the ultimate choice we make. This can, without our even knowing it, distort our decision-making process and lead us to the wrong decision. In Chapter 10, we will show you how to identify and temper the impact of the most common psychological traps.

Bill's story underscores one more important lesson about making smart choices: *take control.* Create your own decision opportunities. Be proactive in your decision making. Look for new ways to formulate your decision problem. Search actively for hidden objectives, new alternatives, unacknowledged consequences, and appropriate tradeoffs. Most importantly, be proactive in seeking decision opportunities that advance your long-range goals; your core values and beliefs; and the needs of your family, community, and employer. Take charge of your life by determining which decisions you'll face and when you'll face them. Don't just sit back and watch what—good or bad—comes your way.

# CHAPTER 2

# Problem

You can make a well-considered, well-thought-out decision, but if you've started from the wrong place—with the wrong *decision problem*—you won't have made the smart choice. The way you state your problem frames your decision. It determines the alternatives you consider and the way you evaluate them. Posing the right problem drives everything else.

You're planning to move to a new city, and you need to find an unfurnished apartment to rent. So your decision problem seems straightforward: Which apartment should I choose? But is it really so simple? Maybe it would actually be in your best interest to rent a house, not an apartment. Or maybe you should put your belongings into short-term storage and rent a furnished apartment for a few months to learn more about the city before committing to a lease. Or maybe you should try to find someone who's looking for a roommate. Or maybe you should just go ahead and buy a condo. In fact, *maybe* you shouldn't move to that city at all.

How you pose a problem profoundly influences the course you choose. The decision you reach from "What city?" will be entirely different from the decision you reach from "Which apartment?". The way you state the problem therefore represents a crucial choice in its own right. Get it wrong and you'll march out in the wrong direction. Get it right and you'll be well on your way to where you really want to go. *A good solution to a well-posed decision problem is almost always a smarter choice than an excellent solution to a poorly posed one.*

## Be Creative about Your Problem Definition

The greatest danger in formulating a decision problem is laziness. It's easy to state the problem in the most obvious way, or in the way that first pops into your mind, or in the way it's always been stated in the past. But the easy way isn't necessarily the best way. To make sure you get the problem right, you need to get out of the box and think creatively.

Many years ago, a struggling West Coast port was reinvigorated because someone posed a decision problem creatively. Every three years, the powerful dock workers' union negotiated a new contract with management. To avoid layoffs, the union had over the years demanded—and been granted—a slew of restrictive work rules. The rules had come to tie management's hands, preventing the adoption of more efficient new technologies for loading and unloading ships. As a result, the port was losing business.

The management bargaining committee, entering a new round of contract negotiations, saw its problem as getting the union to relax some of the more obstructive rules, in exchange for increased wages and benefits. But then a committee member, a consultant from outside the industry, asked a bold question:

"What could management afford to pay the union in a one-time settlement to have *all* the work rules dropped?" The negotiators had never thought of this possibility before, because the existing work rules had constrained their thinking.

The answer to "What could management afford?" depended, of course, on how the port would operate if freed from the work rules. A study, commissioned by the bargaining committee, concluded that the changes would be revolutionary and the savings enormous.

The upshot: the committee negotiated a generous buyout with the dock workers, eliminating the work rules for a price that, though considerable, represented only a fraction of the projected savings. During the years that followed, the port completely changed its mode of operation, adding, among other things, the ability to handle containerized cargo. The results were spectacular. Shipowners benefited—with ship turnaround times cut from days to hours, their ships became far more productive, and their costs plummeted. Consumers benefited, as perishable fruit from Hawaii became cheaper and more plentiful. And, as traffic at the port grew, the workers themselves benefited. More and better jobs became available on the docks.

It was a real breakthrough—all because someone had taken a fresh look at an apparently routine problem and posed it in a creative new way.

## Turn Problems into Opportunities

Decision problems are called "problems" for a reason. Rarely, after all, do we make a decision for the fun of it. We make decisions because we have to deal with difficult or complicated circumstances. We're in a quandary, we're at a crossroads, we're in trouble—and we need to find a way out. But problems aren't always bad. In fact, by stating your problem creatively, you can often transform it into an opportunity, opening up attractive and useful new alternatives. As Albert Einstein said, "In the middle of difficulty lies opportunity." No matter how bad a situation seems, ask yourself: What can I gain from this situation? What are the opportunities here?

U.S. manufacturing companies discovered the bright side of decision problems when they were forced by law to eliminate environmentally harmful materials from their operating processes. At first, the companies saw only the negatives—disruptions, higher costs, more paperwork. But then some of them began to see opportunities. Instead of viewing the problem in its narrow and obvious form—How can we get rid of the harmful materials?—they redefined it more broadly: How can we produce our product in the best and most efficient way? As a result, they made breakthroughs in their operations that have actually enabled them to have lower production costs without toxic materials than with them. By changing a problem into an opportunity, they gained an important advantage over their less-savvy competitors.

In this case, the law acted as a trigger. Every decision problem has a *trigger*—the initiating force behind it. Triggers take many forms. Your boss asks you to choose a new mailing-list software package. A chat with your spouse about ways to use your backyard gives you an idea about new lawn furniture. A friend's heart attack makes you realize that it's finally time to get in shape.

Most triggers come from others (your boss) or from circumstances beyond your control (new regulations affecting your business). Because they're imposed on you from the outside, you may not like the resulting decision problems. But there's no law that says you have to wait for a decision to be forced on you. You can take the initiative. In fact, creating decision situations for yourself is a great way to create new opportunities *before a problem even arises.* You can, for example, review your career path on a regular basis, seeing if you want to move in a new direction. You don't have to wait until you get a lousy raise or your employer runs into trouble or you get a new boss whom you don't get along with. Be proactive. Seek decision opportunities everywhere.

## Define the Decision Problem

So what's the best method for defining—or redefining—your decision problem? Start by writing down your initial assessment of the basic problem, then question it, test it, hone it.

**Ask what triggered this decision.    Why am I even considering it?** The trigger is a good place to start because it is your link to the essential problem. State the trigger as clearly as you can. Include

| | |
|---|---|
| **1.** Your assumption of what the decision problem is. | We need new lawn furniture. |
| **2.** The triggering occasion. | Chat with spouse. |
| **3.** The connection between the trigger and the problem. | How to use our yard. |

As you explore the trigger, beware! Triggers can bias your thinking. They can trap you into viewing the problem only in the way it first occurred to you. When your boss asks you to choose a new mailing-list software package, for instance, the problem might not actually be: What's the best package to buy? The real problem may be: What's the best way to manage our company's direct-mail program? You may find that you don't need new software at all. You need to contract with an outside company to take over the mailing effort.

**Question the constraints in your problem statement.** Problem definitions usually include constraints that narrow the range of alternatives you consider. For example, the problem definition "When should we conduct the three-month market test of our new credit card offering in the Midwest?" assumes (1) that there will be a market test, (2) that it will last three months, and (3) that it will be in the Midwest. Often, such constraints are useful—they focus your choice and prevent you from wasting time wrestling with irrelevant options. Sometimes, though, they put blinders on you, preventing you from seeing the best options. As the following example demonstrates, identifying and challenging the constraints can lead you to better problem definitions and better solutions.

---

### Questioning Constraints: The Berkeley Meeting

A West Coast snowboard manufacturer was getting ready to make a big push into the northeastern U.S. market. To craft its strategy, it appointed a team of three people—one from its headquarters in Berkeley, California; one from its manufacturing plant in Vancouver, British Columbia; and one from its sales office in Denver, Colorado. The vice president of marketing in Berkeley, the head of the team, suggested they get together for a three-day meeting to pull together the final strategy, and he asked his executive assistant to schedule the meeting in Berkeley as soon as possible. After many telephone calls and e-mails, however, the assistant could find no good dates for a three-day meeting any time in the next two months.

Unable to schedule the meeting, the assistant started asking some questions. Was a three-day meeting really necessary, or would two days do? Were all three individuals needed for the entire time? But even scheduling everyone for at least one day proved difficult.

The vice president went back to basics, asking himself and his colleagues, "Why are we considering a meeting at all?" Simple: to complete the strategy. He then asked, "How else can we get the work done?"—in effect recasting the decision problem from "When do we meet?" to "How can we finish the strategy?"

The team came up with a new plan of action. The vice president would outline the steps needed to complete the strategy and would then assign tasks to himself and his two associates. Using e-mail, the team members would update one another on the outcomes of the tasks. Then they would hold three two-hour conference calls over the next two weeks to bring it all together.

The plan worked, and the strategy was solid within three weeks.

---

**Identify the essential elements of the problem.**    If you're an actor and you need to choose your next role, the elements of your decision problem might include any or all of the following: What role will gain me the most exposure? How much money do I need to earn? What's the best way to develop my skills? What are the limits on my time and travel? Should I wait for more options to open up, or should I concentrate on what's available now? By first breaking a problem down into its component pieces, you can be sure that your problem statement is focused on the right goal.

**Understand what other decisions impinge on or hinge on this decision.**    What other decisions will affect this one? What other decisions will this one influence? Whether your company will allocate funds for training may influence how far afield you look for a new word processing package. How much you spend on it may influence what new computer and telecommunications hardware your organization will be able to buy. Rarely does a decision exist in isolation. Thinking through the context of a decision problem will help keep you on the right track.

**Establish a sufficient but workable scope for your problem definition.**    Should related decisions be made part of this decision? Should part of this decision be peeled off and dealt with separately? You need to weigh a comprehensive, broad definition against a more easily tackled, narrower one. An ideal solution for a problem that is too narrow could be a poor solution for a more broadly and accurately defined problem. If you're looking to minimize gasoline costs, you might overinflate your tires to reduce road friction. But if your real problem is cutting your overall automobile operating expenses, this might be a very poor decision. The money you save on gas may be more than offset by the cost of having to replace your tires sooner.

**Gain fresh insights by asking others how they see the situation.** After you've asked, answered, and reviewed all of the above questions to your satisfaction, get some other perspectives. Depending on the nature of the problem, you might seek advice from a family member, a knowledgeable friend, an acquaintance who has faced a similar problem, or a professional in a relevant field. Their ideas will help you see your problem in a new light, perhaps revealing new opportunities or exposing unnecessary, self-imposed constraints. If you can't actually talk to anyone, it can even be worthwhile to imagine how others might think. Ask, for example: How would my accountant see this problem? How would my boss look at it? Don't be afraid to be creative. If you're a politician, you might want to imagine how Harry Truman or Winston Churchill would have thought about the problem you're facing.

## Reexamine Your Problem Definition as You Go

Obviously, you will want to create the best possible problem definition at the outset. But even after putting considerable effort into defining the problem and then digging into its solution, your perceptions may change. You might start off thinking that your problem is planning your summer vacation, only to realize that what really appeals to you is a winter trip to South America. You don't have the time or the money to take two vacations, so you need to change your original problem definition.

Remember that defining your decision problem is itself a decision problem, the resolution of which will profoundly influence your ultimate choice. That's why it's important not only to consider several possible problem definitions in the beginning, but also to pause along the way and reexamine the definition you've chosen. Faced with a competitor that has just made a 20 percent improvement in the clarity of its video conferencing picture, a telecommunications company might at first formulate its decision problem as "How do we match their level of clarity as quickly as possible?" But on further consideration, it might realize that it could actually gain an advantage if it recast the problem as "What technological innovation would allow us to leapfrog the competition by achieving a 100 percent improvement in clarity?"

Chances to redefine your problem are opportunities that often lead to better decisions. So, from time to time as you work your way through the decision-making process, ask yourself: Am I working on the right problem? Questioning the problem is particularly important when circumstances are changing rapidly or when new information becomes available. A poorly formulated decision problem is a trap. Don't fall into it.


## Maintain Your Perspective

If it seems like we're making a big deal out of the problem definition, you're right. Crafting a good definition takes time; don't expect to get it right in one sitting. True, the effort involved in creating a good, comprehensive definition must be balanced against such considerations as time ("I don't have time to address a more complex problem right now"), importance ("The decision's not very important—it's not worth all that effort"), saliency ("I have more pressing matters on my plate"), and emotional energy ("I'm not ready to face that now"). But in 99 out of 100 cases, spending extra time defining the problem pays off handsomely in the end. It increases the odds that you'll make the smart choice.

## A Poor Problem Definition Limits Options:
## Finding a New Job

Bob Hamonski lost his job in Portland, Oregon. Well, sort of. When his company was acquired by a larger one, his position as a financial analyst was eliminated. The new owners were eager to keep Bob, however, and they offered him his choice of financial analyst positions at other subsidiary companies they owned—all in states other than Oregon.

Relocating was problematic because Bob was just concluding a divorce. The divorce agreement, an amicable one, would give him custody of the couple's two young children, while his wife, a lawyer, would pitch in with emergency child care and take the kids on weekends.

Bob could have defined his decision problem in various ways, but he never stopped to think about it. Instead, even though his skills were highly marketable, he proceeded as if his problem were "How do I stay with my current employer?" As a result, he chose one of the open analyst positions—with a subsidiary in Seattle, Washington, the closest option to Portland.

Now, however, Bob's life is a nightmare whenever a child is sick, because his ex-wife is too far away to babysit. And the five-hour round-trip drives to Portland every weekend aren't much fun either. To add insult to injury, the job itself isn't as good as his old one.

With a different problem definition (such as "What's the best financial analyst job I can get in Portland?"), Bob probably would have ended up with a better job with a different employer—without having had to move. By allowing others to frame his decision problem, he unnecessarily narrowed his options.

Too often, people give short shrift to problem definition (as the story of Bob Hamonski above illustrates). In their impatience to get on with things, they plunge into the other elements of decision making without correctly formulating the problem first. Though they may feel like they're making progress in solving their problem, to us they seem like travelers barreling along a highway, satisfied to be going 60 miles an hour—without realizing they're going the wrong way.

## APPLICATION

### To Renovate or Move?

Meet Darlene and Drew Mather. They've run out of space in their two-bedroom, one-and-a-half-bath, finished-basement home, and they have to decide what to do.

Eight years ago, the young couple bought a modest house on School Street in an urban residential neighborhood. Darlene had been pregnant with their son, John, at the time, so they'd left their tiny apartment to give their expected child a room of his own. Now, a second child is on the way. At first, Darlene and Drew had tried to figure out how they might accommodate the new child in the existing house. Could John share his room with the baby? (He'd quickly tire of that.) Could they divide their own bedroom? (A possibility, but their room was already overcrowded.) They quickly came to see that they wouldn't be able to make do with the space they had.

So they've decided to add onto the house, and for the last two months they've been reviewing and pricing their renovation options. A bedroom off the end of their one-story house would cost $25,000, for example, and take away a large chunk of their already-small yard. Adding a second story would save the yard but cost $40,000.

Having bought the house when they did, they've reaped the benefits of a doubling in prices in the local real estate market over the past eight years. A close friend and realtor, Anne Chu, has told them that their house would sell now for $155,000—a pretty good deal, since they originally paid $77,750. With a remaining mortgage of $57,000, their equity totals $98,000 ($155,000 minus $57,000). Their job situations, too, are stable. Darlene works full-time as a nurse in a local hospital, though she plans to work only part-time for a couple of years after the baby is born. Drew works as a salesman and has a secure, solid job. Their joint income before taxes is about $75,000 a year. They feel confident they can afford the renovation—they can use the equity in the house to finance it, and they should have no trouble meeting the monthly payments.

But one evening, after Drew puts the dinner dishes away, Darlene starts a conversation with a thought that will lead them down a new path.

"Drew, John really got me thinking today. You know Jimmy, his friend down the block? Well, Jimmy's family is going to move, so John asked me why people move and when *we* were going to move. At first I thought he was apprehensive that we might move, too. But he was actually excited about the possibility! We had a long conversation about why people move, and the more we talked, the more I got to thinking: Why don't we consider moving instead of renovating?"

"Are you *serious?* In *today's* market?"

"Well, this is a new idea for me, too. But when I rattled off to John the reasons why people move—and he offered reasons, too, like getting more room to play, being able to ride his bike in the street, and being closer to school—I half convinced myself that this might not be such a wild idea. Sure, prices are high, but we've built up a lot of equity in our house, and if we sold it we'd be able to afford a down payment on a bigger one. We'd also avoid $25,000 or more in renovation costs."

Thunderstruck, Drew exclaims, "I can't believe this! For two months now, we've been talking about needing space and renovating. Boy, sometimes it just takes an eight-year-old to set his parents straight! Our real problem isn't 'How should we remodel?' It's 'How do we get enough room for our growing family?' or 'How do we get a better home?' Remodeling our house is only one possibility!"

*(To be continued in Chapter 3.)*

## Lessons from the Application

Darlene and Drew started with an overly narrow problem definition: "How do we renovate?" Their trigger was the need for additional space to accommodate the new baby. At the outset, they didn't stop to think about the different ways to state the problem—they jumped to the conclusion that renovation was their best option. Luckily, John's naive question—"Why do people move?"—got them thinking more broadly. What suggestions might help them now?

- First, they should take more time to reflect on still other possible problem definitions. They might take into account how, for example, a move out to the suburbs would affect their quality of life. Or they might think about whether they'll have a third child in the future or whether there might be an aging relative to house and care for.
- Second, they should identify and examine some of the assumed constraints surrounding their decision and ask themselves whether they might want to loosen, eliminate, or replace some of them. If they moved, for example, how much would it matter if they were farther away from Drew's or Darlene's family? Might they be able to find good jobs with different employers, widening the geographic area available to them?

Expansive thinking generates better problem definitions. And better definitions open up a broader range of creative solutions.

# CHAPTER 3

# Objectives

YOU'VE FORMULATED THE RIGHT DECISION PROBLEM. Now, before you rush into making the actual decision, pause and think hard about your objectives. What do you really want? What do you really need? What are your hopes? your goals? Answering these questions honestly, clearly, and fully puts you on track to making the smart choice.

Why are objectives so important? They form the basis for evaluating the alternatives open to you. They are, in other words, your decision criteria. By making sure you've identified all your objectives, you will avoid making an unbalanced decision—one that, for example, considers financial implications but ignores personal fulfillment. In addition, a full set of objectives can help you think of new and better alternatives, looking beyond the immediately apparent choices.

Objectives are very personal, but they need not be self-centered. Depending on the decision, the objectives you establish can reflect concerns for your family, your employer, your community and country, even the whole of society. Imagine that you're a freelance writer and you've just completed a long assignment writing a computer training manual for a large company. Now you're looking for your next job. Your immediate inclination is to solicit similar work from other big companies—that course would fulfill your objectives for maximizing your income and building your business portfolio. But then you begin to think of other objectives that are also important to you: supporting your community, helping the less fortunate, broadening your experience. You decide to take a lower-paying job writing a fundraising letter and brochure for a local hospice for AIDS patients. Even though you've forgone some income, you soon realize that, by looking beyond your own concerns, you've made a wise decision.

## Let Your Objectives Be Your Guide

Sometimes, the process of thinking through and writing out your objectives can guide you straight to the smart choice—without your having to do a lot of additional analysis. Here's an example. Imagine that your boss has just offered you a promotion. The new job, which requires you to move cross-country from San Diego to New York City, has a considerably higher salary. Your gut reaction is "Great, just what I wanted!" But careful thinking about your full set of objectives gives you reason to hesitate. While the new position would be advantageous financially, the move would disrupt the lives of your spouse, your 12-year-old twin boys, and yourself.

Working with your family, you determine your most important objectives: to promote your family's quality of life, to further your professional development, and to contribute to your firm. When you look back at the offer in light of these objectives, your view changes dramatically. You realize that your family's love of warm weather and outdoor recreation makes it likely that their quality of life would suffer in New York. You see that, although your new position would be challenging and satisfying, it's actually less suited to your talents and interests than your current job. And you decide that your contributions to your firm would be about the same in either position. The money would indeed be better in New York, but maximizing your income, you now see, is only one of your fundamental objectives. Your decision is suddenly clear-cut. You decline the promotion, explaining your reasoning in clear and compelling terms to your boss.

Even when the answer isn't so obvious, the objectives you set will help guide your entire decision-making process, from defining alternatives at the outset, to analyzing those alternatives, to justifying the choice you ultimately make. Specifically:

- **Objectives help you determine what information to seek.**
  You've been offered a job at a new employer. In setting out your objectives, you realize that the work environment is critically important to you. You log on to the Internet and browse through your prospective employer's web site to find out what it indicates about the firm's culture.

- **Objectives can help you explain your choice to others.**   Your boss asks you to justify a recent decision to sign a long-term service contract for your company's photocopying machines. Armed with your list of objectives, you walk her through your thought process, showing how your decision fulfilled the key objectives better than the other alternatives.

- **Objectives determine a decision's importance and, consequently, how much time and effort it deserves.**   If the time of tomorrow's dentist appointment makes little difference in what really matters to you, why fuss over it?

Whenever you feel that your decision process is bogging down or heading off course, always focus back on your objectives. They'll keep you on the right track.

## Watch Out for These Pitfalls

Remember the old saying "If you don't know where you're going, any route will get you there"? Too often, decision makers don't take the time to specify their objectives clearly and fully. As a result, they fail to get where they want to go.

Why? Often, *decision makers take too narrow a focus*. Their list of objectives remains brief and cursory, omitting important considerations that become apparent only after they have made a decision. They concentrate on the tangible and quantitative (cost, availability) over the intangible and subjective (features, ease of use). "Hard" concerns drive out the "soft." In addition, they tend to stress the short term (enjoy life today) over the long term (have a comfortable retirement).

These missteps occur for two main reasons. First, *most people spend too little time and effort on the task of specifying objectives*. They feel they already know what they want and need. Without further reflection, they immediately pick an alternative that seems to "solve" their problem and they move on. Only later, when things turn out less well than anticipated, do they realize that they didn't really understand their objectives after all. By then, of course, it's too late.

Second, *getting it right isn't easy*. Objectives don't just pop up in nice neat lists. While you might think you know what you want, your real desires may actually be submerged—buried beneath the desires others have for you, beneath societal expectations and norms, beneath everyday concerns. For important decisions, only deep soul-searching will reveal what really matters—to *you*. This kind of self-reflective effort perplexes many people and makes them uncomfortable. But the more relentlessly you probe beneath the surface of "obvious" objectives, the better the decisions you'll ultimately make.

## Master the Art of Identifying Objectives

Identifying objectives is an art, but it's an art you can practice systematically. Follow these five steps.

**Step 1: Write down all the concerns you hope to address through your decision.**     Thrash about as much as necessary. Don't worry about being disorganized or mixing up major concerns with ones that seem trivial. This early in the process, too much orderliness will only inhibit your creativity. Use as many ways as you can think of to jog your mind about present, future, and even hidden concerns. Don't worry if you sometimes seem to be saying the same thing in different ways. Rephrasing the same concern may help you uncover important nuances.

Flesh out your list by trying some of these techniques:

- Compose a wish list. Describe as completely as you can everything that you could ever want from your decision. What would make you really happy?

- Think about the worst possible outcome. What do you most want to avoid?
- Consider the decision's possible impact on others. What do you wish for them?
- Ask people who have faced similar situations what they considered when making their decision.
- Consider a great—even if unfeasible—alternative. What's so good about it?
- Consider a terrible alternative. What makes it so bad?
- Think about how you would explain your decision to someone else. How would you justify it? Your answers may uncover additional concerns.
- When facing a joint or group decision, one involving family or colleagues, for instance, first have each person involved follow the above suggestions individually. Then combine the lists, using the varied perspectives to expand and refine first-take ideas. By initially freeing each person to search his or her mind without being limited by others' thoughts, you'll get a more comprehensive list that more accurately reflects everyone's concerns.

Using these techniques and others of your own devising, you'll accumulate pages of notes describing what you most care about in relation to the decision you face.

**Step 2: Convert your concerns into succinct objectives.** The clearest and most easily communicated form for objectives is a short phrase consisting of a verb and an object, such as "Minimize costs," "Mitigate environmental damage," and so on. (For an example of identifying objectives, see the case on pages 35–36.)

## Identifying Objectives: Selecting a Primary School

Mary and Bill needed to select a primary school for their daughter, Kate. To provide a basis for identifying and evaluating the alternatives, each of them made a list of what they felt was important for Kate's education. Then they combined their thoughts, easily completing, after about ten minutes, the following joint list of objectives:

- Learn the fundamentals.
- Enjoy school.
- Develop creativity.
- Develop discipline.
- Learn good work habits.
- Learn to work with other people.
- Participate in physical activity.
- Learn about different people.
- Be intellectually challenged.
- Know the joy of learning and knowledge.
- Participate in and develop an appreciation for art.
- Learn to function in our society.
- Develop options for the future (secondary schools).
- Develop lasting friendships.
- Deepen a commitment to basic values (honesty, helping others, empathy).

They followed the same two-step procedure to compile a second list, this time focusing on what *they* wanted from the school. In combining their two lists this time, however, they found an area of apparent disagreement: Mary had listed "No uniforms" and Bill, "Uniform required."

In discussing their reasons, Mary said, "I hate uniforms for kids. It reminds me of militarization. I think diversity of dress is much healthier."

"But," Bill countered, "you surely don't want competition in dress. It's not fair to the kids who can't afford every new in-thing."

They reconciled their positions by sorting out the *essential* element in each perspective. This effort yielded the following additions to their original list of requirements for a good primary school choice:

- Minimize annual school cost.
- Minimize travel time to school.
- Encourage diversity in styles of life (dress, interests).
- Discourage competitive behavior for material possessions (clothes, bikes).
- Encourage respect for and understanding of all kids, regardless of family circumstances.

---

**Step 3: Separate ends from means to establish your fundamental objectives.**    Having drawn up your initial list of objectives, you now want to organize them. The challenge is to distinguish between objectives that are means to an end (having leather seats in your new car) and those that are ends in themselves (having a comfortable and attractive interior).

Separating means from ends is like peeling an onion. Each new layer looks different. The best way to do it is to follow the advice of the common Japanese saying "You don't really understand something until you ask five times 'Why?'" Simply ask "Why?" and keep asking it until you can't go any further. The U.S. Environmental Protection Agency (EPA), for example, uses the objective "Minimize emissions" for evaluating many proposed programs to reduce air and water pollution. But is this objective an end or a means? Let's ask "Why?" and find out.

*So why do they want to minimize emissions?*

Because it will reduce pollutant concentrations.

*Why is this important?*

It will limit human exposure to the pollutants.

*Why is this important?*

Because exposure can damage people's health.

*And why is health damage an important concern?*

Health damage just *is* important. It's the end the EPA wants to arrive at; everything else is a means of getting there.

Asking "Why?" will lead you to what you really care about— your fundamental objectives, as opposed to your means objectives. *Means objectives* represent way stations in the progress toward a *fundamental objective,* the point at which you can say, "I want this for its own sake. It is a fundamental reason for my interest in this decision." Fundamental objectives constitute the broadest objectives *directly* influenced by your decision alternatives.

Consider this example. Your initial notes on developing a plan for constructing your company's new distribution center include the objectives "Minimize construction time" and "Minimize time needed to get permits." You ask yourself "Why?" and realize that these are means objectives; they lead to the two fundamental objectives "Minimize time before the distribution center is operational" and "Minimize cost of the facility."

Your fundamental objectives depend on your decision problem. A means objective in one decision problem may be a fundamental objective in another. Suppose you've just turned 55, and you plan to retire in ten years, at 65. You face two related decision problems: how to invest your retirement funds now and what to do during your retirement years. In the first case, a fundamental objective would be to accumulate as much money as possible for your retirement. In the latter case, having money is only a means objective. Asking several "Why?s" will lead you to the fundamental objective: achieve and maintain a good quality of life.

Separating means and fundamental objectives is critical because both kinds of objectives play important but different roles in the decision-making process:

- **Each means objective can serve as a stimulus for generating alternatives and can deepen your understanding of your decision problem.**   Asking how you might minimize construction time for the distribution center, for example, could lead to several good alternatives for shortening the time before the distribution center is operational, such as moving all needed construction materials immediately to the site.

- **Only fundamental objectives should be used to evaluate and compare alternatives.**   Sure you want to do better in terms of your means objectives. But why? Only to do better in terms of your fundamental objectives. If you use a fundamental objective *and* its supporting means objectives to evaluate decision alternatives, you will give too much weight to that particular fundamental objective in your final choice.

**Step 4: Clarify what you mean by each objective.**   You should at this point have a solid list of fundamental objectives. Now, for each fundamental objective, ask "What do I really mean by this?" Asking "What?" enables you to clearly see the components of your objectives. Clarification will lead to better understanding, which in turn will help you to state the objective more precisely and see more clearly how to reach it. In addition, when it comes time to choose, you'll be better prepared to appraise whether or not the objective is being met.

For many objectives, the bottom-line meaning will be obvious. "Minimize cost," for example, means just that: spend the least possible number of dollars. The meaning of other objectives can be more elusive. You want to "Minimize damaging health effects" from a certain air pollutant. But exactly which health effects? And to whom? You might want to "Maximize prestige" in your professional field. But what do you mean by prestige? In whose eyes? Clarifying the meaning of an objective will help you achieve it.

**Step 5: Test your objectives to see if they capture your interests.** Having clarified each of your objectives, it's time to test them. Use your list to evaluate several potential alternatives, asking yourself if you would be comfortable living with the resulting choices. If not, you may have overlooked or misstated some objectives. Re-examine them. A second useful test is to see if your objectives would help you explain a prospective decision to someone else. If using your objectives as reasons and explanations would be difficult, you probably need to spend more time refining the objectives. What's unclear? What's missing?

## Practical Advice for Nailing Down
## Your Objectives

You will more readily identify your fundamental objectives if you keep the following considerations in mind.

**Objectives are personal.**   Different people facing identical situations may have very different objectives. For example, a single person investing for retirement may care only about a mutual fund's long-term value, whereas a married person might also care about the fund's interim value, as it would help support her family in case of her early death.

**Different objectives will suit different decision problems.**   People tend to forget this obvious point. (It's easier, after all, to recycle objectives than to reformulate them for each decision.) Hospitals should use different objectives when hiring a chief fundraiser, for example, than when hiring a chief financial officer.

**Objectives should not be limited by the availability of or ease of access to data.**   Many people mistakenly focus on immediate, tangible, measurable qualities when listing objectives, but these may not reflect the essence of the problem. Using easy-to-measure but only partially relevant objectives is like looking for a lost wallet under a streetlight because there's more light there, even though you know you lost the wallet around the corner in a dark alley. Easily measurable objectives won't always illuminate what really matters. Watch out for this trap!

**Unless circumstances change markedly, well-thought-out fundamental objectives for similar problems should remain relatively stable over time.**   The key phrase here is "well-thought-out." Clearly, with deeper reflection, objectives will change if they were not carefully derived in the first place. But given thoughtful objectives and an absence of major changes in health, finances, and so on, fundamental objectives for similar problems will remain the same or change only slowly.

**If a prospective decision sits uncomfortably in your mind, you may have overlooked an important objective.**   Such late discoveries may strike you as a sign of sloppy thinking, but that isn't always the case. Sometimes you must stare a decision in the face before a previously unrecognized objective leaps out. Consider this example. A committee established by a local school board was asked to organize a day-long citizens' conference on the future of the town's schools. The committee drafted an agenda using a list of objectives set by the board. To the committee's dismay, however, the board rejected it. Even though the agenda met all of the board's specified objectives, further discussion revealed a previously unrecognized objective: avoid topics that were divisive. The board saw this objective only when it was confronted with a decision about the meeting agenda, which contained controversial topics.

## APPLICATION

### To Renovate or Move?

Drew and Darlene Mather now have two possibilities for getting adequate space for their growing family: to renovate or move.

"OK," Drew says, "if we're really serious about this, let's draw up lists of why we should move and why we shouldn't. What do we really want?"

Darlene takes out a pad and pencil, and after about an hour of lively discussion, she has filled up a couple of pages with their ideas. During

## What We Want in a House

| Objectives | Subobjectives |
|---|---|
| 1. Good location | Commute time for Drew |
| | Commute time for Darlene |
| | Distance to school for John |
| | Distance to shops |
| 2. Quality of school | |
| 3. Quality of neighborhood | Crime |
| | Traffic |
| | Playgrounds |
| | Athletic facilities (swimming pool, tennis courts, bike path) |
| 4. Quality of house | Size (number of bedrooms, bathrooms) |
| | Kitchen |
| | Family room |
| | Required maintenance |
| | General aesthetics |
| 5. Yard | Size |
| | Landscaping (trees, lawn, garden) |
| 6. Cost | |

this conversation, their son, John, appears and, seeing what they're doing, contributes a few ideas of his own.

The next day, Darlene organizes her notes into a list: "What We Want in a House." Through further discussion, the Mathers refine their list of concerns (they called them objectives), arriving at the set shown above. Satisfied with the result, Darlene and Drew decide they are ready to begin looking to see whether there are houses on the market that would better fulfill their objectives than their current residence would, once renovated.

(*To be continued in Chapter 4.*)

## Lessons from the Application

The Mathers did a lot of things right in thinking through their concerns and translating them into a list of objectives. They took the time to write them down, and they pushed themselves to define their main objectives in terms of their subobjectives. Their process might have been improved, however, if they had followed these guidelines in working up their list:

- For joint or group decisions, first have each individual draw up a list separately, then combine them.
- Phrase each concern as a true objective, using a verb and an object.
- Ask "Why?" for each objective. The Mathers are presumably concerned about crime and traffic because they are concerned about safety. By specifically listing "Maximize safety" as a fundamental objective, other safety issues—steep stairs, retaining walls, and so on—might emerge as important means objectives.
- Ask "What do we really mean by this?" This question will lead to a better understanding of such concerns as, in the Mathers' case, cost and school quality. Does "Cost" refer to the sale price, the size of the down payment and other up-front costs, the size of the mortgage, or the monthly cost for mortgage payments, taxes, improvements, maintenance, and insurance? Similarly, "Quality of school" has many components, and to make meaningful assessments and comparisons, the Mathers will need to define exactly what school quality means to them.

Once the Mathers have more clearly defined their objectives, the following suggestions would help them further refine their list:

- Visit and evaluate some homes currently on the market *before* finalizing the objectives. This step would help the Mathers verify and extend their understanding of their initial objectives.
- Imagine the purchase or rejection of a few different houses and consider how well or easily these choices could be explained to others using the stated objectives.
- Be alert to the possible emergence of an important unrecognized objective, such as a house's potential to appreciate in value.

CHAPTER 4

# Alternatives

Aₗₜₑᵣₙₐₜᵢᵥₑₛ ₐᵣₑ ₜₕₑ ᵣₐw ₘₐₜₑᵣᵢₐₗ of decision making.
They represent the range of potential choices you'll have for pursuing your objectives. Because of their central importance, you
need to establish and maintain a high standard for generating alternatives. Two important points should be kept in mind at all
times. First, *you can never choose an alternative you haven't considered.*
A terrific house in a great neighborhood may be available for
rent, but if you're unaware of it, you won't end up there. Second,
*no matter how many alternatives you have, your chosen alternative can be
no better than the best of the lot.* Thus the payoff from seeking good,
new, creative alternatives can be extremely high.

## Don't Box Yourself In with Limited Alternatives

Unfortunately, people don't tend to think a lot about their decision alternatives. Just as they assume they know their objectives

(even when they don't), so they assume they know the options open to them. Too many decisions, as a result, are made from an overly narrow or poorly constructed set of alternatives. Although the common denominator in all these cases is lack of thought, the essential problem can take many forms.

One of the most common pitfalls is *business as usual*. Because many decision problems are similar to others that have come before, choosing the same alternative beckons as the easy course. It's Friday after work, and you and your date are trying to decide what to do. You went to dinner and a movie the last six Fridays. Hey, how about dinner and a movie? Last year's city budget assigned 40 percent to schools, 30 percent to the police and fire departments, 20 percent to social services, and 10 percent to recreation, maintenance, and other activities. Why not make the same allocations this year? Business as usual results from laziness and an overreliance on habit. With only a modest amount of effort, attractive new alternatives can usually be found.

But, sometimes so-called new alternatives represent nothing more than *incrementalizing*—making small and usually meaningless changes to previously devised alternatives. This year's city budget may differ from last year's, but only by a few percentage points, more or less. Don't just tweak the status quo. Step back and develop alternatives that reflect fresh thinking and different perspectives.

Many poor choices result from falling back on a *default alternative*. Say you're a recent college graduate with a degree in marine sciences, a field you love, but you're being pressured to return to the Midwest to join the family clothing business. You haven't got any job offers in marine sciences (perhaps because you haven't looked that hard). You feel trapped, so you take the family job—

the default alternative. Remember, every decision problem has multiple alternatives, even if it doesn't seem to at first. What people really mean when they say, "No alternatives" is "No alternatives better than the default option"—*yet*. Creating fresh alternatives requires some focused thinking.

Choosing the *first possible solution* is another pitfall. Suppose you've recently moved and need to select a local physician. You ask a coworker for the name of her doctor, and you make an appointment. You embrace the first alternative—the easy choice. Although efficient, the process was not thorough and as a result could backfire. There's nothing, after all, that says the easy choice will be the smart choice. The coworker's doctor may be competent, but he may not have the communication skills, the hospital affiliation, the certification, the referral network, or the office hours that would best meet your needs. With a little extra effort, you would no doubt be able to find a doctor who met *your* criteria. Develop a new habit: once you find one possible solution, look further—generate new alternatives that could lead to a *better* solution.

Choosing among *alternatives presented by others* can also result in a poor decision. You're happily employed. Then one day the phone rings and a corporate recruiter makes you an attractive job offer with another company. What do most people do? They choose between the current job and the proposal, both of which have been shaped or presented by others. But if you are willing to consider leaving your current job, why not actively seek still other alternatives? Don't get boxed in.

People who wait too long to make a decision risk *being stuck with what's left* when they finally do choose. The best alternatives may no longer be available. If you delay choosing among vacation plans, for example, all the best flights may be full by the time you're ready to make reservations. If you delay dealing with a health problem, your condition may have deteriorated so much by the time you act that your options are limited. Remember, get an early start on major decisions. Take charge.

## The Keys to Generating Better Alternatives

Generating a good set of alternatives isn't all that difficult, but it takes time and thought. Try some of these techniques to make the most of your efforts:

**Use your objectives—ask "How?"**    Since your objectives drive your decisions, use them to guide your search for good alternatives. Ask yourself "How can I achieve the objectives I've set?" Do this separately for each individual objective, including both means objectives and fundamental objectives.

Asking "Why?" took you from means to ends; asking "How?" will take you from ends back to means, leading you toward alternatives. After all, alternatives are the ultimate means. You're planning a new distribution center. *How* would you fulfill the fundamental objective "Minimize the time before the center is operational"? One answer: by minimizing the time needed to get construction permits. *How?* By hiring a local attorney who knows local regulations and local bureaucrats. This is an alternative.

**Challenge constraints.**    Many decision problems have constraints that limit your alternatives. Some constraints are real, others are assumed. Let's say you're in the market for a new car, and you've found a model you really love. There's a problem, though. The car's 18 feet long, and your garage is only 17 feet. The length of the garage is a *real constraint*. With a little creativity, however, you can often find ways around real constraints. You could extend your garage by two feet, for example, or you could park elsewhere.

An *assumed constraint* represents a mental rather than a real barrier. A marketing position opens up in your company. The traditional practice is to promote from within, appointing a current employee without even looking for outside candidates. The traditional practice is an assumed constraint, and in identifying alternatives, it should be ignored (even if you'll need to take it into account as an objective when you ultimately make a decision). To ensure that you examine all viable alternatives, you need to break free from the straitjackets of tradition and habit.

Try assuming that a constraint doesn't exist, and then create alternatives that reflect its absence. If the resulting alternatives are attractive enough, maybe you can figure out how to make them feasible. A utility company, for example, assumed that its proposed new power plant had to be on a waterway to ensure a sufficient supply of cooling water. Working within this constraint, it found that all of its alternatives would cost more than $1.5 billion and would result in significant environmental damage. Under pressure from environmentalists, the utility removed the waterway constraint and took a fresh look at its alternatives. Freed from its self-imposed straitjacket, it identified an inland site that required pumping water a modest 12 miles. The result: a $1.2 billion facility that caused only minimal environmental damage.

**Set high aspirations.**   One way to increase the chance of finding good, unconventional alternatives is to set targets that seem beyond reach. High aspirations force you to think in entirely new ways, rather than sliding by with modest changes to the status quo.

In the late 1980s, for example, many companies sought to lower costs by reducing the size of their support staffs. A common aspiration was a 15 to 20 percent cost reduction. By automating formerly manual processes, some companies managed to lay off enough people to cut their costs by the desired amount. They were delighted—until they heard about competitors who had set cost-reduction goals of 50 percent and had met them. Forced to think in new ways, these companies outsourced some of their support functions entirely, transforming their corporate structures. Setting high aspirations stretches your thinking.

**Do your own thinking first.**   Before consulting others about alternatives, give your own mind free rein. Some of your most original ideas, born of innocence, may be suppressed if exposed to others' ideas and judgments before they have been fully formed. Sometimes ignorance is bliss, so let loose your own creativity for a while. Once you buy into another person's line of thinking, especially someone expert in the matter at hand, your own thoughts may be prematurely knocked out of the running. Noted MIT professor Norbert Wiener, one of the most creative geniuses of the twentieth century, always spent time thinking through a new scientific problem on his own before reading the existing academic literature.

**Learn from experience.**   You shouldn't let yourself be constrained by history, but you should certainly try to learn from it.

Find out what others have done in similar situations, and if you've faced similar decisions before, consider again the alternatives you devised then. (Don't, however, limit your alternatives to those previously considered—you don't want to fall into the "business as usual" trap.) For example, if you're looking for ideas on how to remodel your house, you might go on a tour of recently remodeled houses in your community.

**Ask others for suggestions.**   After you've thought carefully about your decision and your alternatives on your own, you should then seek the input of others to get additional perspectives. People at a distance from a problem may see it more clearly, without the conceptual or emotional blocks that you may have. (See the career choice example below for an example of using advice to overcome constraints.) In seeking out advice, consider people in fields beyond the obvious. For ideas on keeping track of hospital surgical supplies, for example, you might ask the parts manager at a local car dealership how they track their inventory.

Keep an open mind during these conversations. The primary benefit may not be the specific ideas that others provide, but simply the stimulation that *you* get from talking about your decision, from organizing your thoughts into explanations, and from answering questions. It may well be you who ends up generating the most valuable ideas.

---

**Identifying New Alternatives:**
**Making a Better Career Choice**

Many years ago, we counseled a British student who was near the top of his class at Harvard Business School. His tuition was paid by a British chemical company, for which he had formerly worked as an engineer, with the understanding that after graduation he would return to the company. At the time, the company had a rigid career policy: Engineers remained as engineers for a fixed period before they could become managers.

The student was dismayed, because since he was an engineer, his hard-won new business skills would go unused and unnoticed. Furthermore, his salary would be less than a third what his classmates were being offered. He was tempted by the challenges and financial rewards of a management consulting career, but he also felt obligated to fulfill his arrangement with his former employer. What should he do?

We were able to suggest an alternative he hadn't considered: pursue management consulting opportunities, but at the same time approach your former employer and state your concerns, offering to repay your tuition. They may respond by rethinking your placement and salary. if not, move on—take a management consulting job and reimburse the chemical company.

The company did offer a much-improved position and salary, but one that the student still found far less suitable than management consulting. The student accepted a consulting job and 25 years later was head of European operations for a major international consulting firm. (The chemical company, by the way, graciously declined his offer of reimbursement and wished him well.) Getting an outside perspective helped the student challenge assumed constraints and create an alternative that freed him from his dilemma.

---

**Give your subconscious time to operate.**    How many times have you had a great idea while drifting off to sleep or taking a shower?

Your subconscious had been turning over the problem, and a good idea bubbled up in a quiet moment. The subconscious needs time and stimulation to do this well. Start thinking about your decision problem as soon as possible; don't put it off until the last minute. Once you've begun, make a point of thinking about the problem from time to time to give your subconscious a nudge. Your reward may well be a flash of insight. (Always write these insights down quickly when they occur; details are easily forgotten.)

**Create alternatives first, evaluate them later.**   Creating good alternatives requires receptivity—a mind expansive, unrestrained, and open to ideas. One idea leads to another, and the more ideas you entertain, the more likely you are to find a good one. Bad ideas will almost certainly emerge along with good ones. That's a necessary part of the process and something you shouldn't be concerned about at this point. Don't evaluate alternatives while you're generating them. That will slow the process down and dampen creativity. An obvious shortcoming, even a potentially fatal flaw, should not keep you from listing an alternative. If some aspect of the alternative is promising enough, it may be worth the effort to try to eliminate the inadequacy later. Evaluation narrows the range of alternatives. At this stage, your task is to broaden the range by bringing forward as many alternatives as possible.

**Never stop looking for alternatives.**   As the decision process moves on to the consideration of consequences and tradeoffs, the evaluation stages, your decision problem will become increasingly clear and more precisely defined. Often, the evaluation will turn up shortcomings in your existing alternatives, which may in turn suggest better ones. Keep your mind and your eyes open.

Here's a case in point. Public officials had to decide whether to approve the construction of a natural gas terminal at Matagorda Bay, Texas. There were a number of alternatives for the terminal's location and design, but even the best of them carried a small risk of a serious accident that could cause fatalities in nearby communities. Analysis found that most of the risk fell on summer weekends, when the bay was crowded with pleasure boats and the beaches thronged with sunbathers. Based on the analysis, the best alternative in contention was modified in a simple way: ship operations at the terminal would be suspended on summer weekends. The revised alternative reduced the public risk by 75 percent, with essentially no drawbacks.

## Tailor Your Alternatives to Your Problem

Just as certain cuts and styles of clothing suit certain people, certain kinds of alternatives fit certain kinds of decision problems. When, for example, uncertainty and risk play a major role in determining the consequences of a decision, as in most investment decisions, you may want to seek alternatives that reduce risk through such means as diversification and hedging. (We'll talk more about risk in Chapter 8). Four categories of alternatives—process, win-win, information-gathering, and time-buying—are particularly well suited to specific kinds of problems.

**Process alternatives.**     Odd as it may seem, the best alternative is sometimes a *process* rather than a clear-cut choice. Suppose your two roommates, Heidi and Susan, are both big fans of figure skating, and you arrive home one evening to find an answering machine message from your sister saying that she has an extra ticket for the National Ice Skating Championships. She knows that you have plans for that evening, so she offers to give the ticket to one of your roommates. It's up to you to decide who gets it. The basic alternatives are clear—give the ticket to Heidi or to Susan—but the choice is tough. One answer is simply to flip a coin—heads, Heidi goes; tails, Susan does. The coin toss is a process alternative—it establishes a process for deciding who will get the ticket. You all consider the coin toss to be fair, whereas the risk of making the choice yourself (angering a roommate) is great. Hence, it is clear to you that the process alternative is the best alternative.

Process alternatives help to ensure the fairness of decisions involving conflicting interests and thus can help preserve and foster long-term relationships. Other familiar process alternatives include the following:

- Voting
- Binding arbitration
- Standardized test scores (to establish minimum requirements)
- Sealed bids
- Auctions

To create process alternatives, you can begin by listing all of the basic alternatives from which to choose (for example, a slate of candidates to chair a committee). Then you should determine the right process mechanism (such as a secret ballot) for selecting the best alternative. In other situations, such as binding arbitration, the alternatives won't be clearly specified before-

hand. The process itself both creates the basic alternatives and selects one.

**Win-win alternatives.**    Sometimes devising great alternatives isn't
the problem. The problem is that your decision requires someone else's approval. Suppose you've decided to ask for a three-
month leave of absence from your job at a pharmaceutical
company in order to take advantage of a once-in-a-lifetime opportunity: volunteering at a remote hospital in Africa. Your boss,
the decision maker, must approve your leave, which he is not
inclined to do. To change his mind, you need to create an alternative that will address his concerns as well as fulfill your own
objectives.

The key is to step back and analyze *his* decision problem. What
are his objectives, and how can you use them to create a win-win
alternative that benefits both of you? Suppose that your boss has
been assigned responsibility for developing a new procedure for
appraising your company's product quality. He's uncomfortable
with the task because he feels he lacks the right analytical back-
ground. You, on the other hand, feel well suited to the job. You
offer your boss a deal: you'll create and implement the procedure
over the next six months, putting in a lot of nights and weekends,
if he'll then grant you the leave. He agrees—you both win.

Making someone else's decision-problem alternatives jibe with
your own—creating a win-win alternative—is like lighting two
candles with one match. It's economical, it's satisfying, and it gets
the job done.

**Information-gathering alternatives.**    Information helps dispel the
clouds of uncertainty hovering over some decisions. A doctor,

for example, will gather information from a patient's history, examination, and tests to reduce uncertainty about a diagnosis. A business will test a prototype of a new product to ensure that it meets all performance expectations. Better information means better decisions.

When there are uncertainties affecting a decision, it is useful to generate alternatives for gathering the information necessary to reduce each uncertainty. First list the areas of uncertainty. Then, for each one, list the possible ways to collect the needed information. Each of these ways is an information-gathering alternative. Sometimes the alternatives are well established, with predictable costs and accuracy—comparison shopping and medical tests are two examples. In other cases, you'll need to design an information-gathering alternative tailored to your particular needs, evaluating, for example, the relative merits and cost-effectiveness of a telephone poll, a direct-mail survey, and a market test.

**Time-buying alternatives.**   "Don't put off 'til tomorrow what you can do today." That's a good rule for decision making, but as with most rules, there are times when you should break it. Deferring a decision can provide you with additional time to better understand a decision problem, gather important information, and perform complex analyses. You may, as a result, be able to dispel uncertainties and reduce risks. Sometimes, extra time may allow you to create a new alternative that is much better than all the current alternatives.

Deferring a decision usually comes at a price, however. Some alternatives may disappear in the interim. Several used cars you had been looking at, for example, may be sold by the time you return to the lot. Other alternatives may erode. Delaying the release of a new product while you explore the market, for example, may allow the competition to get in first.

Devising a halfway alternative, a partial commitment, can sometimes circumvent the drawbacks of a delay in making a full commitment. A family uncertain about spending its summers in Maine, for example, may decide to lease a vacation home there for two years, reserving an option to buy at a set price. The lease, a time-buying alternative, gives them a chance to determine whether they really like the house and area before committing to ownership.

Whenever you're uncomfortable about deciding now, question the deadline. Is it a real deadline, or is it just an assumed constraint? What would be the pros and cons of waiting? If the pros outweigh the cons, look for a time-buying alternative. But beware! Make sure the deferral offers real benefits. Don't use it merely to avoid an unpleasant or tough decision.

## Know When to Quit Looking

It's an unfortunate truth: *the perfect solution seldom exists.* But that doesn't stop a lot of people from endlessly (and unrealistically) pursuing one. It's important to be careful and thorough in laying out your alternatives. Obsessing over them, though, is a different matter. It takes a heavier toll in time and in mental and emotional energy than is justified.

How will you know when enough is enough? You need to balance the effort made against the quality of the alternatives found. To strike the right balance, ask yourself these questions:

- Have you thought hard about your alternatives, using the techniques listed on pages 48–54?
- Would you be satisfied with one of your existing alternatives as a final decision?
- Do you have a range of alternatives? Are some alternatives distinctly different from the others? (If your alternatives all seem too similar, you need to push your creativity.)
- Do other elements of this decision (such as consequences and tradeoffs) require your time and attention?
- Would time spent on other decisions or activities be more productive?

If you answered "yes" to each of these questions, stop looking for more alternatives and apply your energies elsewhere.

**APPLICATION**

### To Renovate or Move?

Darlene and Drew have thought hard about their objectives, and, list in hand, they are ready to look for alternatives.

Darlene proposes calling Anne, their realtor friend, but Drew counters, "Shouldn't we first try on our own? Maybe we can even avoid the realtor's commission."

John pipes up: "I'll ride my bike around the neighborhood and look for 'For Sale' signs."

"You will not," his mother scolds. "You know you aren't allowed to ride your bike in the streets."

But John has another idea. "Well, I could announce in my class that we're looking for a new house and offer a reward."

"No, John, you'll do no such thing. We don't want to tell the world we want to move before we're sure we can afford to."

The next few weeks are hectic. In their few available free hours, Darlene and Drew answer newspaper ads, and the family visits houses that sound promising. Often, though, the advertised homes don't meet their expectations. John wants to know when they will quit looking and decide. "I don't know when, John," his dad says, "but I know not yet."

Frustrated and exhausted with the time-consuming search process, Darlene and Drew at last decide to call Anne. But their do-it-yourself efforts do pay a small dividend: the process has helped them to sharpen their thinking about what they really want and to bring their aspirations more in line with reality.

The following week, Darlene and Anne meet for lunch. As they eat dessert, Anne summarizes their discussion. "Let's see. You and Drew want to buy a house that's close to each of your jobs. You want the finest of schools for John and for the precocious kid you're about to have. You want to live in a quality neighborhood. You want more than adequate living space and a big yard for the kids and for the dog you've always wanted. And you want all of this to be affordable and a very good investment. You also want me to arrange for the Federal Reserve to lower interest rates so you can get a 5 percent mortgage. You want me to sell your old house for an above-market price. And because we're such good friends, you want me to accept 4 percent rather than the standard 6 percent commission."

"I never said anything about your commission, Anne."

"But you were thinking it."

"How could you tell?"

"I'm not psychic, but I am an observer of human behavior, and four of my last five clients, who all knew me slightly in high school, asked me for that favor—which I politely told them I couldn't do because I promised to send my own kids to college."

As they leave the restaurant, Anne quips, "If your John wants a job in my real estate office, tell him to come around. This is the first time I know of that a kid has helped his parents formulate their housing problem."

Over the next few weeks, the Mathers pore over listings and visit many houses. Several meet a lot of their objectives, but Drew and Darlene don't put in any bids. The family is in a search phase, trying to get a feel for the possible.

Then Anne phones one night. "Time for action, folks. You can't be voyeurs all your lives. How about putting your money on the line?"

Darlene and Drew acknowledge that they've seen enough and that now is the time to buy. John heartily agrees. One morning he tells his mother that if they don't do something soon his new brother won't have a place to sleep.

So Darlene pulls out her list of viable alternatives. The house on Eaton Street has a yard big enough for a dog. The Wade Street house has the best school district of the lot. The West Boulevard house is sort of crummy, but a terrific buy. The house on Amherst is a bit distant, but the neighborhood is stable, with great amenities. Finally, their own house at 281 School Street needs some renovations but is a decent default option.

"So what do we do now?" asks Drew.

"How do we decide?" asks John.

(*To be continued in Chapter 5.*)

### Lessons from the Application

The Mathers have done a good job of generating alternatives, first by answering ads on their own (even if it was a rather inefficient and ultimately ineffective method) and then by enlisting the aid of a realtor. Could they have done better? We think so. Darlene and Drew might have benefited from the following suggestions:

- Consider your objectives and, for each, ask "How?" By evaluating neighborhoods first, for example, the Mathers could have narrowed their search, ruling out locations that did not meet key objectives such as school quality and commuting time. They might have saved a lot of time by only visiting homes on the most fertile ground.

- Be proactive in creating alternatives. The Mathers could have asked friends or friends of friends in attractive neighborhoods to alert them if a house was about to come on the market. They might also have placed a newspaper ad themselves, specifying what they were looking for in a house, rather than merely responding to others' ads. This would accomplish what John had wanted to do by making an announcement to his classmates, but in a broader sphere and in a more discreet way.

- Think carefully about the right time to stop looking for new alternatives and make a decision. This is often a challenge. The Mathers were pushed by their realtor, who took the initiative to say, "It's time to decide." By quickly agreeing, they avoided further searching, but it may have been wiser to think twice. Only the actual decision makers can truly say when and if they are ready to make a choice.

One more thing to keep in mind as we move on: never irrevocably commit yourself to considering only existing alternatives. The Mathers have five houses on the table. But they should continue looking while they evaluate these. They may reject all five after further analysis or unsuccessful offers, and they'll want to have more options available.

# CHAPTER 5

# Consequences

You've defined your problem, you've structured your objectives, and you've established the set of alternatives you have to choose from. Now, to make a smart choice, you need to compare the merits of the competing alternatives, assessing how well each satisfies your fundamental objectives. To make the comparisons, you'll first need to describe how well you'll fare with each alternative. In other words, you'll need to lay out the *consequences* each alternative would have for each of your objectives. If you describe the consequences well, your decision will often be obvious—without requiring much further reflection.

This chapter presents a simple message: *be sure you really understand the consequences of your alternatives before you make a choice. If you don't, you surely will afterwards, and you may not be very happy with them.* The main benefit to be derived from describing consequences is understanding. You will gain a better understanding not only of the consequences themselves, but also of your objectives and even of your decision problem. The more deeply you understand these, the more likely you are to make a smart choice.

## Describe Consequences with Appropriate Accuracy, Completeness, and Precision

Here's a seemingly straightforward problem: You need to decide where to dine before you go to the theater tonight. You want a nice meal in a pleasant setting, you don't want to spend too much money, and most of all, you don't want to be late for the show—you know you'll have only an hour and a half to eat and get to the theater. You've identified two alternatives: Mario's reportedly offers outstanding food but only a fair setting, and the service can be slow. Luigi's, on the other hand, has reasonably good food, a superb setting, and efficient service, but it is the more expensive of the two. Neither alternative offers everything you want—that's the way life is—so your choice will depend on how well each meets your objectives and on the relative importance you assign to those objectives. If you've adequately described the consequences of your two alternatives, you will be in a position to make a smart choice.

Simple, right? Wrong. Describing consequences isn't as easy as it might at first appear. In fact, it can be downright difficult. If your descriptions are inaccurate, incomplete, or imprecise, the three biggest pitfalls, you risk making a poor choice. You won't get what you thought you would. In terms of the restaurant choice, for example, your descriptions may fall short in a number of ways:

- **Inaccurate:** What if, contrary to what you've heard, Luigi's food is actually better than Mario's?

- **Incomplete:** What if Luigi's is 15 minutes farther from the theater than Mario's? What if Mario's doesn't have a liquor license, and you expect to have wine with your dinner?

- **Imprecise:** How slow is Mario's service? How much more expensive is Luigi's?

When we think about the challenge of defining consequences, we're reminded of an old joke about a now-defunct airline that was known for its erratic service. When one of this airline's flights touched down one day, the pilot came on the intercom. "We're early," he announced, "but we're lost." If you don't define the consequences well, you may arrive at a decision quickly, but it probably won't be the right choice.

## Build a Consequences Table

The trick is to describe the consequences with enough precision to make a smart choice, but not to go into unnecessary and exhausting detail. How do you master this trick? By taking these four steps:

**Step 1: Mentally put yourself into the future.** Because the consequences of your decisions will occur in the future, often months or years from now, you need to shift your mindset ahead in time to uncover a decision's true significance. As you think about each alternative, instead of imagining you *might* choose it, imagine that you *have* chosen it. Imagine, for example, that you *have* remodeled your house following the plans just submitted by your architect. Ask yourself what life is like in the remodeled house. What is a typical weekday like? a weekend day? a summer day? a winter day? What's it like when you have house guests? How are things different when your children are three years older? Putting yourself in the future will help you to focus on the longer-term consequences of a decision rather than just the immediate ones, and it will help you to view those consequences in their actual context.

**Step 2: Create a free-form description of the consequences of each alternative.** Write down each consequence using the words and numbers that best capture its key characteristics.

- Gather hard information (for example, the résumé of a job candidate), but also express your subjective judgments (the candidate is "eager" or "personable").
- Use numbers where appropriate (the candidate's desired salary is $37,000); otherwise, use words ("extensive computer and analytical skills"). Use graphics—diagrams, photos, symbols—if they are revealing and can be used consistently (you might use a suitcase icon, for example, to indicate the candidate's willingness to travel).
- Check your description against your list of objectives. Do your descriptions take into account all your objectives? If you've missed any, you will need to fill in the gaps. Does any of your descriptions imply a previously unstated objective? If so, you will want to evaluate its appropriateness and, if it is to be retained, apply it to your other alternatives. (The possibility of turning up unrecognized objectives makes starting with a free-form description of consequences preferable to describing them using your objectives as a checklist.)

**Step 3: Eliminate any clearly inferior alternatives.** This step is a terrific time saver for many decisions because it can quickly eliminate alternatives and may lead to a resolution of your decision. You essentially play "king of the mountain," trying to knock one alternative out with another.

- Take two alternatives. Select one as the tentative king. The status quo, if it is one of the alternatives, often makes a good initial king. For example, you start by comparing your current computer to one of the new models you're thinking about buying.
- Use your descriptions to identify the pros (in one list) and the cons (in another) of the king in relation to the second alternative, making sure you cover each objective. If one alternative emerges as clearly superior, eliminate the other and use the survivor as the king for your next comparison. If neither is eliminated, retain the second alternative and continue your comparisons using your original king.
- Continue through your list of alternatives, comparing them in pairs. At the end of the process, one alternative may emerge as the clear selection. If not, continue to the next step.

**Step 4: Organize descriptions of remaining alternatives into a consequences table.**    Using pencil and paper or a computer spreadsheet, list your objectives down the left side of a page and your alternatives along the top. This will give you an empty matrix. In each box of the matrix, write a concise description of the consequence that the given alternative (indicated by the column) will have for the given objective (indicated by the row). You'll likely describe some consequences quantitatively, using numbers, while expressing others in qualitative terms, using words. The important thing is to use consistent terminology in describing all the consequences for a given objective—in other words, use consistent terms across each row. Now, compare pairs of alternatives again, and eliminate any that are inferior.

If your choice is now obvious, congratulations! If not, you're going to have to make tradeoffs, a task we'll describe in detail in the next chapter. In any case, the consequences table you've developed will be an essential tool for evaluating contending alternatives.

## Compare Alternatives Using a
## Consequences Table

To illustrate the power and usefulness of a consequences table, let's examine one created by a young man named Vincent Sahid. The only child of a widower, Vincent plans to take time off from college, where he's majoring in business, to help his father through a serious illness. To make ends meet while away from school, he will need to take a job. He wants a position that pays adequately, has good benefits and vacation allowances, and involves enjoyable work, but he'd also like to gain some experience that will be useful when he returns to school. And, given his dad's illness, it is important that the job give him the flexibility to deal with emergencies. After a lot of hard work, Vincent identifies five possible jobs. Each has very different consequences for his objectives, and he charts these consequences as shown on page 69.

As you can see, a consequences table puts a lot of information into a concise and orderly format which allows you to easily compare your alternatives, objective by objective. It gives you a clear framework for making comparisons and, if necessary, tradeoffs. Moreover, it imposes discipline, forcing you to bring together all your thinking about your alternatives, your objectives, and your consequences into a single, concise framework. Although this kind of table isn't too hard to create, we're always surprised at how rarely decision makers take the time to put down on paper

## Consequences Table for Vincent Sahid's Job Decision

| Objectives | Alternatives | | | | |
|---|---|---|---|---|---|
| | *Job A* | *Job B* | *Job C* | *Job D* | *Job E* |
| **Monthly salary** | $2,000 | $2,400 | $1,800 | $1,900 | $2,200 |
| **Flexibility of work schedule** | Moderate | Low | High | Moderate | None |
| **Business skills development** | Computer | Manage people, computer | Operations, computer | Organization | Time management, multiple tasking |
| **Vacation (annual days)** | 14 | 12 | 10 | 15 | 12 |
| **Benefits** | Health, dental, retirement | Health, dental | Health | Health, retirement | Health, dental |
| **Enjoyment** | Great | Good | Good | Great | Boring |

all the elements of a complex decision. Without a consequences table, vital information can be overlooked and comparisons can be made haphazardly, leading to wrong-headed decisions.

## Master the Art of Describing Consequences

As in all aspects of decision making, there's a good amount of art involved in adequately describing consequences. To improve your practice, try these techniques.

**Try before you buy.**    We use this memorable saying to urge you to *experience* the consequences of an alternative before you choose it, whenever this is feasible. If you're considering buying a van after having always owned sedans, rent one for a week or borrow a friend's. By experiencing the consequences first hand, they become more meaningful. In addition, you're likely to identify consequences you hadn't even thought of before. Maybe you'll discover that it's difficult to park the van in your small parking space at work, but that, on the other hand, your elderly father has a much easier time getting in and out of it.

There are lots of ways to try before you buy. If you're considering a particular college, you can stay overnight on campus, eat in the dining hall, attend some classes, and socialize with the students. You can drive a prospective commuting route between your job and a new house you're considering buying. You can build a prototype or create a computer image of a new toaster you're designing.

**Use common scales to describe the consequences.**    Sometimes, verbal descriptions of consequences, however well organized, won't be sufficient to resolve a decision problem. In these cases, scales will enable you to describe consequences more clearly and to make otherwise difficult decisions more easily.

To be useful, scales must represent measurable, meaningful categories that capture the essence of your objective. Measures such as dollars (for income or the cost of products), percentages (for on-time flights), or acres (for wildlife habitat preserved) clearly have these characteristics, but how could you measure more intangible qualities, such as corporate goodwill, organizational morale, or pain and suffering? There are two possibilities:

- Select a meaningful scale that captures the essence of the corresponding objective. One of Vincent Sahid's job objectives is flexibility of work schedule. His consequences table shows a general assessment of this factor, but how might he measure it more precisely? For his decision, the percentage of scheduled work hours that can be rearranged without authorization may be an appropriate scale.
- Construct a subjective scale that directly measures your objective. You regularly make or accept decisions based on subjective scales: the A to F grade scale used in schools; the green-circle, blue-square, black-diamond ratings for the difficulty of ski slopes; and the Standard & Poors financial risk ratings for bonds. To construct a scale yourself, you need to define concretely as many levels as are needed to distinguish significant differences in consequences. Sometimes even a simple two-point scale will do (as when noting whether or not prescription drugs will be required for a given medical treatment alternative).

Trying as they may be, such struggles with difficult-to-measure objectives yield a significant benefit: determining how you would measure an objective forces you to clarify what you really mean by it.

**Don't rely only on hard data.**    By all means use hard data whenever they are reliable, consistent, and relevant. But don't gravitate toward hard data simply because they seem "objective" or easy to obtain.

- Give due recognition to objectives that can't be measured by hard data. In deciding where to locate a highway, for instance, don't ignore the minimization of visual degradation in favor of the minimization of cost merely because the latter can be measured by hard data.

- Choose scales that are relevant, regardless of the availability of hard data. The last thing you want is an irrelevant scale. Better to choose "daily commute time" as a scale in determining where to live, rather than the more easily measurable but less revealing "distance from work."

**Make the most of available information.**   Sometimes hard data will be readily available, as they were when Vincent Sahid documented the salaries of his possible employment opportunities. At other times, no data will be available, and you'll need to go with your judgment alone, as Vincent did in describing how well he might enjoy the various jobs. For some cases, though, you'll have a little data, but you'll need to supplement it with judgment—as well as a good dash of logic. Suppose you were considering different itineraries for a four-week trip of a lifetime for your family to Australia and New Zealand. All other things being equal, one of your objectives would likely be to minimize the overall cost of the trip, which would require estimating a number of different cost components. For airfares, you could get accurate data. For hotel costs, you'd likely use your judgment about the class of hotel that you would typically stay in and gather some recent data about the average rates of such hotels. Meal costs might be based on your travel agent's best judgment. You would also need to use a good deal of judgment in estimating the costs of activities you'll pursue during the course of the trip. There may be data available on some of these costs, but others will require educated guesses. Finally, you'll need to add up all the costs—this is where the logic comes in—to get an estimate of the total itinerary cost.

**Use experts wisely.** Frequently, others—we'll call them "experts"—will know more about the possible consequences than you do. Accountants and tax attorneys can best assess the ramifications of putting investments in your name or your child's name. And your nine-year-old may be the family expert on how much a particular birthday present would please an eight-year-old cousin.

When you seek out the judgment of others, be sure you understand not just the consequences they project but how they derived those consequences. You will want a full explanation of the underlying data, judgments, and logic. This explanation will be especially important for controversial decisions that you will need to explain or justify to family, colleagues, or others.

**Choose scales that reflect an appropriate level of precision.** Too often, the terms used in describing consequences imply a level of precision that is higher or lower than is reasonable or useful. A rough cost estimate stated as "$33,475" implies too much precision in the scale. It would be more accurate if it were stated as "$33,000 ± 10 percent."

In other cases, people make the opposite error of introducing scales that *understate* the accuracy of an estimate. They do this in the interest of simplicity, but in the process they mask meaningful differences. In one instance of such an error, state highway engineers screened hundreds of bridges to be included in a five-year upgrade and repair program. Their initial cost estimates for each bridge, which ranged from $0.5 million to $20 million, were accurate only to ± 20 percent. Worried about the lack of precision, the engineers created a three-point scale to compare costs: *A* indicated "inexpensive," *B* indicated "moderately expensive," and *C* indicated "expensive." Unfortunately, these categories reflected such wide ranges of costs that they masked the level of accuracy that had already been attained. The range indicated by a *B* rating, for example, ran from $3 million to $10 million, making the initial 20 percent variations look trivial.

**Address major uncertainty head on.**   For some consequences, you won't be certain about what will happen. When the uncertainty is modest, you can usually define consequences using an estimate or a representative figure. When comparing new cars to buy, for example, you won't know the actual prices until you negotiate a purchase, but a reasonable estimate will serve to narrow the field or even to make a choice. In this and in many other cases, the low uncertainty level will not influence the decision. For many other decisions, however, uncertainty may loom large enough to complicate your ability to describe consequences adequately. With decisions involving investments, insurance, or complex medical or legal matters, you will want to address the uncertainties explicitly—a topic we'll address in Chapter 7.

APPLICATION

### To Renovate or Move?

The Mather family is ready to submit a bid—but for which house and for how much? To help them decide, Darlene and Drew review their notes on each of their five alternative houses, organizing them into lists of pros and cons. The resulting pages of notes for each house overwhelm Drew, however, and he protests, "This is too much detail for me—I need to see the comparisons on a single sheet of paper. We know what we're looking for in terms of objectives—school, commuting time, all that. How well do the houses stack up against each other on each of those objectives?"

Darlene agrees that they need a more accessible format. Using her original list of "What We Want in a House" (Chapter 3) and her notes, Darlene clarifies their objectives by going into more detail on some subobjectives. As a result, she puts together a new table, which compares the consequences for each house in terms of each of their six objectives. Darlene lists down the left side of her paper the objectives and subobjectives, and across the top, the five houses being considered. In some rows she describes the consequences in words (such as "Poor," "Pretty good," and "Wonderful" for playgrounds), and in others she uses numbers (such as for commuting times and size of yard).

For their current School Street house, the Mathers and their realtor determine a fair equivalent "Asking price," $175,000, assuming that an additional bedroom were added to the end of their house. The task of laying out the consequences is time consuming, but it's worth it to Darlene, who feels that this is one of the biggest decisions the family will make.

She proudly shows her effort to her husband. "You wanted one sheet, so here's one sheet." (See pp. 76–77.)

Drew is duly impressed. He needs further explanations of some of Darlene's terse descriptions, but once he understands the entries in the table, he agrees with them. Even John understands the table.

The table is useful—Drew and Darlene eliminate Eaton Street on the basis of its poor showing—but a final choice still eludes them.

(*To be continued in Chapter 6.*)

## Lessons from the Application

The Mathers have made a lot of progress toward selecting a house. Thanks to Darlene's efforts, they can easily compare the houses in terms

# Consequences Table for the Mathers' New House

| Objectives | Subobjectives | *Amherst* |
|---|---|---|
| Good location | Commute time for Drew (one way) | 40 min. erratic |
| | Commute time for Darlene | 25 min. heavy |
| | Distance to school for John | Bus 10 min. |
| | Distance to shops | Needs car, 5 min. |
| Quality of school | % scoring above state norm | 90 |
| | Basics (reading, math, science) | Very good |
| | Music program | Good |
| | Athletic program | Superb |
| | High school quality | Very good |
| Quality of neighborhood | Crime | Some |
| | Traffic | Quiet street |
| | Playgrounds | Wonderful |
| | Athletic facilities | Excellent |
| | Kids close by | Some |
| | Neighbors | New friends |
| Quality of house | Bedrooms | 4, 2 small |
| | Bathrooms | Great |
| | Kitchen | A pleasure |
| | Family room | Adequate |
| | Required maintenance | Good shape |
| | General aesthetics | Pleasant |
| Yard | Size | 3,000 sq. ft. |
| | Garden (trees, shrubs) | Fine shape |
| | Suitability for dog | OK |
| | Suitability for kids | Perfect |
| Cost | Asking price | $225,000 |
| | Real estate taxes | $3,500/year |
| | Other concerns | Low maintenance |
| | | Growth in equity |

**Alternatives**

| Eaton | School | Wade | West Boulevard |
|---|---|---|---|
| 30 min. heavy | 20 min. | 15 min. | 30 min. |
| 20 min. moderate | 25 min. light | 20 min. | 15 min. |
| Bus 10 min. | Walk, 2 blocks | Walk, 5 min. | Walk, 4 blocks |
| Needs car, 3 min. | Easy walk | Easy walk | Long walk |
| | | | |
| 65 | 55 | 95 | 70 |
| Passable | Poor | Very good | Good |
| Fine | None | Excellent | Just OK |
| Poor | Very good | Good | Good |
| Good | Good | First-rate | Good |
| | | | |
| Moderate | Low | Little | Mod. to high |
| Mod. rush hours | Moderate | Mod. rush hours | Mod. to high |
| So-so | Adequate | Pretty good | Poor |
| Adequate | Fine | Adequate | Good |
| Very few | Lots | Lots | Just a few |
| Bothersome | Congenial | Compatible | Seem nice |
| | | | |
| 4 small | 3 small | 3 large | 3 average |
| Adequate | Not good | Good | A problem |
| Good | Good | Nice | Best part of house |
| Pitiful | Fine | Large, fireplace | Small |
| Fine shape | Poor shape | Needs work | Mod. |
| Just OK | Poor | Pleasant | OK to good |
| | | | |
| 5,000 sq. ft. | 1,500 sq. ft. | 4,000 sq. ft. | 2,000 sq. ft. |
| Pedestrian | Awful | Needs work | Needs attention |
| Great | Not good | Good | Poor |
| Good | So-so | Fine | Poor to OK |
| | | | |
| $240,000 | $175,000 | $195,000 | $180,000 |
| $3,200/year | $2,200/year | $2,500/year | $2,300/year |
| — | High maintenance with renovation | Mod. maintenance | — |

of the consequences for their objectives. While the consequences table doesn't reveal an obvious choice, it does allow the Mathers to drop one alternative (Eaton Street) from further consideration, as it is clearly inferior to at least one other house and therefore a poor choice.

At this stage, the Mathers might benefit from the following suggestions:

- Identify or construct scales for some objectives. Scales would both clarify the meaning of some objectives and facilitate comparisons among the remaining alternatives. Take "Crime," for example. Are the Mathers concerned with violent crime against people, with property crime, with vandalism, or with all of the above? Are data available on the annual incidents of each type of crime for each neighborhood? Can the Mathers create a crime index for each neighborhood? If crime is a major concern, it would be worth taking this step. At the very least, discussing how they would measure crime would clarify their concerns, even if they don't actually create a crime index.
- Check all consequences for accuracy and stability. John, a third grader, may now have a 5-minute walk to his primary school, but if the walk to the local middle school, which John will attend in three years, is 20 minutes, using 5 minutes as a consequence description would be inaccurate. The Mathers may need to think a little bit further into the future.
- Check all consequences for completeness. The consequences describing school quality for John's middle school are missing; they should be defined for all of the prospective houses.
- Check the precision of all consequences. The description "Needs work" for the objective "Garden (trees, shrubs)" for example, leaves a lot of room for interpretation. Better to include an estimate of the time or dollar cost for the work.
- Systematically compare the remaining alternatives, two at a time. List the pros and cons of each relative to the others. Easier than comparing four alternatives all at once, pair-at-a-time comparisons often identify an alternative that can be dropped and sometimes bring to light new information that points to a single best alternative. At the least, they would help further clarify the relative strengths and weaknesses of the remaining alternatives.

# CHAPTER 6

# Tradeoffs

At this point in the process, having compared the consequences of your alternatives, you will likely have eliminated some poor choices. Those that remain will seem to nearly balance each other: *alternative* A *will be better than alternative* B *on some objectives, but worse on others.* Important decisions usually have conflicting objectives—you can't have your cake and eat it, too—and therefore you have to make tradeoffs. You need to give up something on one objective to achieve more in terms of another.

In the early 1980s, for example, the United States enacted a national speed limit of 55 miles per hour to reduce gasoline consumption. The limit also led to a reduction in highway fatalities. Ten years later, however, a fresh debate broke out over the limit. Proponents pointed to the thousands of lives that had been saved. Opponents argued that with the oil crisis long past and today's cars more fuel-efficient, the national limit should be raised to allow drivers to get to their destinations more quickly. Some participants in the debate held that states should be free to set their own speed limits.

Each of these viewpoints stresses a different objective: lives saved, convenience, and states' rights. Finding an appropriate balance among them is difficult, but not trying to balance them misses the point. Suppose we all agreed that the 55 mile-per-hour limit was justified by the number of lives saved. Inevitably, a proposal for a 45 mile-per-hour limit, clearly preferable given an exclusive focus on saving lives, would quickly follow. Why not 35 miles per hour, then, or 20? Each reduction in the speed limit would, after all, save many additional lives. At some point, however, other objectives would come into play. The vast majority of people would not accept a speed limit of 20 miles per hour. They would, in fact, object strenuously, using such reasons as convenience or states' rights, or both. There's the rub. *Decisions with multiple objectives cannot be resolved by focusing on any one objective.*

When you do have only one objective, your decision is straightforward. If you wanted to fly from New York to San Francisco as cheaply as possible, for example, you'd simply find the airline offering the lowest fare and buy a ticket. But having only one objective is a rare luxury. Usually, you're pursuing many different objectives simultaneously. Yes, you want a low fare, but you also want a convenient departure time, a direct flight, and an airline with an outstanding safety record. And you'd also like to have an aisle seat and earn frequent flyer miles in one of your existing accounts. Now the decision is considerably more complicated. Because you can't simultaneously fulfill all your objectives, you're forced to seek a balance among them. You have to make tradeoffs.

Making wise tradeoffs is one of the most important and most difficult challenges in decision making. The more alternatives you're considering and the more objectives you're pursuing, the more tradeoffs you'll need to make. The sheer volume of tradeoffs, though, isn't what makes decision making so hard. It's the fact that each objective has its own basis of comparison. For one objective you may compare the alternatives using precise numbers or percentages—34 percent, 38 percent, 53 percent. For another, you may need to make broad relational judgments—high, low, medium. For another, you may use purely descriptive terms—yellow, orange, blue. You're not just trading off apples and oranges; you're trading off apples and oranges and elephants.

How do you make tradeoffs among such widely disparate things? That's what we're going to show you in this chapter.

## Find and Eliminate Dominated Alternatives

The first step is to see if you can rule out some of your remaining alternatives before having to make tough tradeoffs. The fewer the alternatives, the fewer the tradeoffs you'll need to make and the easier your decision will be. To identify alternatives that can be eliminated, follow this simple rule: if alternative *A* is better than alternative *B* on some objectives and no worse than *B* on all other objectives, *B* can be eliminated from consideration. In such cases, *B* is said to be *dominated* by *A*—it has disadvantages without any advantages.

Say you need a break and want to take a relaxing weekend getaway. You have five places in mind, and you have three objectives: low cost, good weather, and short travel time. In looking at your options, you notice that alternative *C* costs more, has worse weather, and requires the same travel time as alternative *D*. Alternative *C* is dominated and can therefore be eliminated.

You need not be rigid in thinking about dominance. In making further comparisons among your options, you may find, for example, that alternative *E* also has higher costs and worse weather than alternative *D* but has a slight advantage in travel time—it would take a half hour less to get to *E*. You may easily conclude that the relatively small time advantage doesn't outweigh the weather and cost disadvantages. For practical purposes, alternative *E* is dominated by *D*—we call this "practical dominance"—so you can eliminate alternative *E* as well. By looking for dominance, you've just made your decision much simpler—you have to choose among only three alternatives, not five.

Consequences tables, which we discussed in the last chapter, can be great aids in identifying dominated alternatives because they provide a framework that facilitates comparisons. But if there are many alternatives and objectives, there can be so much information in the table that it becomes hard to spot dominance. Glance back at Vincent Sahid's consequences table on page 69, and you'll see what we mean. To make it easier to uncover dominance, you should create a second table in which the descriptions of consequences are replaced with simple rankings.

Working row by row—that is, objective by objective—you determine the consequence that best fulfills the objective and replace it with the number 1; you then find the second best consequence and replace it with the number 2; and you continue in this way until you've ranked the consequences of all the alternatives. When Vincent looks at the "Vacation" objective in his table, for example, he sees that 15 days ranks first, 14 days ranks second, the two 12 days tie for third, and 10 days ranks fifth. When he moves from the quantitatively measured objectives to the qualitatively measured ones, he finds that more thought is required, as the rankings need to be based on subjective judgments rather than objective comparisons. In assessing the benefits packages, for example, he decides that dental coverage is more important to him than a retirement plan, and he makes his rankings on that basis. Vincent's ranking table is shown below.

Dominance is much easier to see when you're looking at simple rankings. Vincent sees that job *E* is clearly dominated by job *B*—it's worse on four objectives and equivalent on two. Comparing job *A* and job *D*, he sees that job *A* is better on three objectives and worse on one (vacation), with two ties. When an alternative has only one advantage compared to another, as with job *D*, it is a candidate for elimination due to practical dominance. In this case, Vincent easily concludes that the one-day vacation advantage of job *D* is far outweighed by its disadvantages in salary, busi-

### Ranking Alternatives on Each Objective for Vincent Sahid's Job Decision

| Objectives | Alternatives | | | | |
|---|---|---|---|---|---|
| | *Job A* | *Job B* | *Job C* | *Job D* | *Job E* |
| **Monthly salary** | 3 | 1 | 5 | 4 | 2 |
| **Flexibility of work schedule** | 2 (tie) | 4 | 1 | 2 (tie) | 5 |
| **Business skills development** | 4 | 1 | 3 | 5 | 2 |
| **Vacation (annual days)** | 2 | 3 (tie) | 5 | 1 | 3 (tie) |
| **Benefits** | 1 | 2 (tie) | 5 | 4 | 2 (tie) |
| **Enjoyment** | 1 (tie) | 3 (tie) | 3 (tie) | 1 (tie) | 5 |

ness skills development, and benefits. Hence, job *D* is practically dominated by job *A* and can also be eliminated.

Using a ranking table to eliminate dominated alternatives can save you a lot of effort. Sometimes, in fact, it can lead directly to the final decision—if all your alternatives but one are dominated, then the remaining alternative is your best choice. The process of determining dominance also protects you from mistakenly selecting inferior alternatives, because they are removed from contention.

## Make Tradeoffs Using Even Swaps

If you still have more than one alternative in contention, you'll need to make tradeoffs. At this point, it will be useful to take a short trip back in time to see what the American sage Ben Franklin had to say about decision tradeoffs. More than 200 years ago, Franklin's friend Joseph Priestley, a noted scientist, faced a tough decision, and he wrote to Franklin to ask which of two alternatives he should choose. Franklin recognized that the choice would depend on Priestley's objectives and on his evaluation of the two alternatives with respect to those objectives. Rather than suggest a specific choice, therefore, Franklin outlined a reasonable *process* to help Priestley choose. Here is Franklin's letter, sent from London on September 19, 1772.

> Dear Sir,
>    In the affair of so much importance to you, wherein you ask my advice, I cannot, for want of sufficient premises advise you what to determine, but if you please I will tell you how.

When those difficult cases occur, they are difficult, chiefly because while we have them under consideration, all the reasons pro and con are not present to the mind at the same time; but sometimes some set present themselves, and at other times another, the first being out of sight. Hence the various purposes or inclinations that alternately prevail, and the uncertainty that perplexes us.

To get over this, my way is to divide half a sheet of paper by a line into two columns; writing over the one pro, and over the other con. Then during three or four days consideration, I put down under the different heads short hints of the different motives, that at different times occur to me, for or against the measure.

When I have thus got them all together in one view, I endeavor to estimate their respective weights; and where I find two, one on each side, that seem equal, I strike them both out. If I find a reason pro equal to two reasons con, I strike out the three. If I judge some two reasons con, equal to some three reasons pro, I strike out the five; and thus proceeding I find at length where the balance lies; and if, after a day or two of further consideration, nothing new that is of importance occurs on either side, I come to a determination accordingly.

And, though the weight of reasons cannot be taken with the precision of algebraic quantities, yet when each is thus considered, separately and comparatively, and the whole lies before me, I think I can judge better, and am less liable to make a rash step, and in fact I have found great advantage from this kind of equation, in what may be called moral or prudential algebra.

Wishing sincerely that you may determine for the best, I am ever, my dear friend, yours most affectionately.

*B. Franklin*

Ben Franklin proposed a wonderful way to simplify a complex problem. Each time he eliminated an item from his list of pros and cons, he replaced his original problem with an equivalent but simpler one. Ultimately, by honing his list, he revealed a clear choice. Although Franklin did not explicitly use a list of objectives, his caution in advising his friend "for want of sufficient premises," together with his focused approach to his lists of pros and cons, shows that he relied on them implicitly.

A consequences table can be used to extend Franklin's ideas about a "moral or prudential algebra" to a choice among any number of alternatives, not just two. In the following pages, we'll show how to make tough tradeoffs and use them to replace your complex decision problem with a simpler one, just as Franklin did. We call this technique the *even swap method*. First we'll describe how the even swap method works, illustrating the process using a simple example with only two alternatives and two objectives, and later we'll apply it to a more complex situation with many objectives and alternatives.

## The Essence of the Even Swap Method

What is the even swap method? To explain the concept, we need to first state an obvious but fundamental tenet of decision making: if all alternatives are rated equally for a given objective—for example, all cost the same—then you can ignore that objective in choosing among those alternatives. If all airlines charge the same fare for the New York–San Francisco flight, then cost doesn't matter. Your decision will hinge only on the remaining objectives.

The even swap method provides a way to adjust the consequences of different alternatives in order to render them equivalent in terms of a given objective. Thus this objective becomes irrelevant. As its name implies, an even swap increases the value of an alternative in terms of one objective while decreasing its value *by an equivalent amount* in terms of another objective. In essence, the even swap method is a form of bartering—it forces you to think about the value of one objective in terms of another. If, for example, American Airlines charged $100 more for a New York–San Francisco flight than did Continental, you might swap a $100 reduction in the American fare for 2,000 fewer American frequent flyer miles. In other words, you'd "pay" 2,000 frequent flyer miles for the fare cut. Now, American would score the same as Continental on the cost objective, so cost would have no bearing in deciding between them. Whereas the assessment of dominance enables you to eliminate alternatives, the even swap method allows you to eliminate objectives. As more objectives are eliminated, additional alternatives can be eliminated because of dominance, and the decision becomes easier.

## Application of the Even Swap Method

Let's apply the even swap method to a fairly simple problem to illustrate how it works. Imagine you're running a Brazilian cola company, and a number of other companies have expressed interest in buying franchises to bottle and sell your product. Your company currently has a 20 percent share of its market, and it earned $20 million in the fiscal year that's just ended. You have two key objectives for the coming year: increase profits and expand market share. You estimate that franchising would reduce your profits to $10 million due to startup costs, but it would increase your share to 26 percent. If you don't franchise, your profits would rise to $25 million, but your share would increase to only 21 percent. You put all of this down in a consequences table (see below).

Which is the smart choice? As the table indicates, the decision boils down to whether the additional $15 million profit from not franchising is worth more or less than the additional 5 percent market share from franchising. To resolve this question, you can apply the even swap method following a straightforward process.

*First, determine the change necessary to cancel out an objective.* If you could cancel out the $15 million profit advantage of not franchising, the decision would depend only on market share.

*Second, assess what change in another objective would compensate for the needed change.* You must determine what increase in market share would compensate for the profit decrease of $15 million. After a careful analysis of the long-term benefits of increased share, you settle on a 3 percent increase.

*Third, make the even swap.* In the consequences table, you reduce the profit of not franchising by $15 million, while increasing its market share by 3 percent, to 24 percent. The table below

## Consequences Table for Cola Company's Possible Marketing Strategies

| | Alternatives | |
| Objectives | Franchising | Not Franchising |
| --- | --- | --- |
| Profit (in millions) | $10 | $25 |
| Market share | 26% | 21% |

shows the restated consequences (a $10 million profit and a 24 percent market share) that are equivalent in value to the original consequences (a $25 million profit and a 21 percent market share).

*Fourth, cancel out the now-irrelevant objective.* Now that the profits for the two alternatives are equivalent, profit can be eliminated as a consideration in the decision. It all boils down to market share.

*Finally, eliminate the dominated alternative.* The new decision, while equivalent to the original one, is now easy. The franchising alternative, better on market share, is the obvious choice.

For the cola company, only one even swap revealed the superior alternative. Usually it takes more—often many more. The beauty of the even swap approach is that, no matter how many alternatives and objectives you're weighing, you can methodically reduce the number of objectives you need to consider until a clear choice emerges. The method, in other words, is iterative. You keep switching between making even swaps (to eliminate objectives) and identifying dominance (to eliminate alternatives) until only one alternative remains.

## Cola Company's Even Swap

| | Alternatives | |
|---|---|---|
| **Objectives** | *Franchising* | *Not Franchising* |
| **Profit (in millions)** | $10 | $~~25~~  $10 |
| **Market share** | 26% | ~~21%~~  24% |

## Simplify a Complex Decision with Even Swaps

Now that we've discussed each step of the process, let's apply the whole thing to a more complex problem. Alan Miller is a computer scientist who started a technical consulting practice three years ago. For the first year he worked out of his home, but with his business growing he decided to sign a two-year lease on some space in the Pierpoint Office Park. Now that lease is about to expire. He needs to decide whether to renew it or move to a new location.

After considerable thought about his business and its prospects, Alan defines five fundamental objectives for an office: short commuting time, good access to clients, good office services (clerical assistance, copy machines, faxes, mail service), sufficient space, and low cost. He surveys more than a dozen possible locations and, dismissing those that clearly fall short of his needs, settles on five viable alternatives: Parkway, Lombard, Baranov, Montana, and his current building, Pierpoint.

He then develops a consequences table (page 91), laying out the consequences of each alternative for each objective and using a different measurement scale for each objective. He describes commuting time as the average time in minutes needed to travel to work during rush hour. To measure access to clients, he determines the percentage of his clients whose business is within an hour's lunchtime drive of the office. He uses a simple three-point scale to describe the office services provided: *A* means full service, including copy and fax machines, telephone answering, and for-fee secretarial assistance; *B* indicates fax machines and telephone answering only; and *C* means that no services are available. Office size is measured in square feet, and cost is measured by monthly rent.

## Consequences Table for Alan's Office Selection

| | Alternatives | | | | |
| Objectives | *Parkway* | *Lombard* | *Baranov* | *Montana* | *Pierpoint* |
|---|---|---|---|---|---|
| **Alan's commute (min.)** | 45 | 25 | 20 | 25 | 30 |
| **Client access (%)** | 50 | 80 | 70 | 85 | 75 |
| **Office services (constructed scale)** | A | B | C | A | C |
| **Office size (sq. ft.)** | 800 | 700 | 500 | 950 | 700 |
| **Monthly cost (dollars)** | 1,850 | 1,700 | 1,500 | 1,900 | 1,750 |

To simplify his decision, Alan immediately seeks to eliminate some alternatives by using dominance or practical dominance. To make this easier, he uses the descriptions in the consequences table to create a ranking table (page 92).

Scanning the columns, he quickly sees that the Lombard office dominates the current Pierpoint site, outranking it on four objectives and tying it on the fifth (office size). He eliminates Pierpoint from further consideration. He also sees that Montana almost dominates Parkway, falling behind in cost only. Can he eliminate Parkway, too? He flips back to his original consequences table and notices that, for the small cost disadvantage of Montana—only $50 per month—he would gain an additional 150 square feet, a much shorter commute, and much better client access. He eliminates Parkway using practical dominance.

Alan has reduced his choice to three alternatives—Lombard,

### Ranking Alternatives on
### Each Objective for
### Alan's Office Selection

| Objectives | Alternatives | | | | |
|---|---|---|---|---|---|
| | *Parkway* | *Lombard* | *Baranov* | *Montana* | *Pierpoint* |
| Alan's commute (min.) | 5 | 2 (tie) | 1 | 2 (tie) | 4 |
| Client access (%) | 5 | 2 | 4 | 1 | 3 |
| Office services (constructed scale) | 1 (tie) | 3 | 4 (tie) | 1 (tie) | 4 (tie) |
| Office size (sq. ft.) | 2 | 3 (tie) | 5 | 1 | 3 (tie) |
| Monthly cost (dollars) | 4 | 2 | 1 | 5 | 3 |

Baranov, and Montana—none of which dominates any other. He redraws his consequences table (see "Redrawn Table," page 93).

To further clarify his choice, Alan needs to make a series of even swaps. In scanning the table, he sees the similarity among the commuting times for the three remaining alternatives. If the Baranov's 20-minute commute were increased to 25 minutes using an even swap, all three alternatives would have an equivalent commute time, and that objective could then be dropped from further consideration. Alan decides that this 5-minute increase in Baranov's commute time can be compensated for by an 8 percent increase in Baranov's client access, from 70 to 78 percent. He makes the swap, rendering commute time irrelevant in his deliberations (see "Eliminate Commute" table, page 93). Alan then checks this table for dominated alternatives but finds none.

## Making a Series of Even Swaps to Select the Right Office

| | Redrawn Table | | | Eliminate Commute | | |
|---|---|---|---|---|---|---|
| | **Alternatives** | | | **Alternatives** | | |
| Objectives | Lombard | Baranov | Montana | Lombard | Baranov | Montana |
| Alan's commute (min.) | 25 | 20 | 25 | ~~25~~ | ~~20~~ 25 | ~~25~~ |
| Client access (%) | 80 | 70 | 85 | 80 | ~~70~~ 78 | 85 |
| Office services (constructed scale) | B | C | A | B | C | A |
| Office size (sq. ft.) | 700 | 500 | 950 | 700 | 500 | 950 |
| Monthly cost (dollars) | 1,700 | 1,500 | 1,900 | 1,700 | 1,500 | 1,900 |

Alan next eliminates the office services objective by making two even swaps with monthly cost. Using the Lombard service level ($B$) as a standard, he swaps an increase in service level from $C$ to $B$ for Baranov for a $250 increase in monthly costs. He also swaps a decrease in service level from $A$ to $B$ for Montana for a savings of $100 per month (see "Eliminate Office Services and Baranov" table, page 94).

Each time Alan makes an even swap, he changes the way the alternatives match up. With the office services objective eliminated, he finds that the Baranov alternative is now dominated by the

## Making a Series of Even Swaps to
## Select the Right Office (continued)

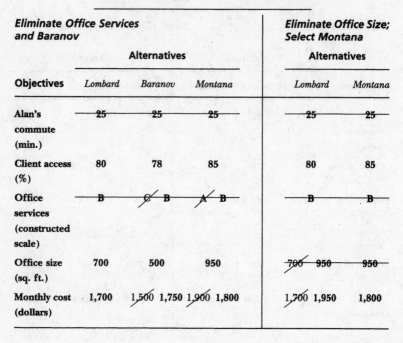

| | **Eliminate Office Services and Baranov** | | | | **Eliminate Office Size; Select Montana** | |
| | **Alternatives** | | | | **Alternatives** | |
| **Objectives** | *Lombard* | *Baranov* | *Montana* | | *Lombard* | *Montana* |
| Alan's commute (min.) | ~~25~~ | ~~25~~ | ~~25~~ | | ~~25~~ | ~~25~~ |
| Client access (%) | 80 | 78 | 85 | | 80 | 85 |
| Office services (constructed scale) | ~~B~~ | ~~Ø B~~ | ~~A B~~ | | ~~B~~ | ~~B~~ |
| Office size (sq. ft.) | 700 | 500 | 950 | | ~~700~~ 950 | ~~950~~ |
| Monthly cost (dollars) | 1,700 | ~~1,500~~ 1,750 | ~~1,900~~ 1,800 | | ~~1,700~~ 1,950 | 1,800 |

Lombard alternative and can be eliminated. This highlights an important process consideration. In making even swaps, you should always seek to create dominance where it didn't exist before, thus enabling you to eliminate an alternative. In your decision process, you will want to keep switching back and forth between examining your columns (alternatives) and your rows (objectives), between assessing dominance and making even swaps.

With Baranov out of the picture, only Lombard and Montana remain. They have equivalent scores in commuting time and services, leaving only three objectives to consider. Alan next makes

an even swap between office size and monthly cost. Deciding that
the 700-square-foot Lombard office will be cramped, he swaps an
additional 250 square feet for a substantial cost increase—$250
per month. This swap cancels the office-size objective, revealing
Montana to be the clearly preferable alternative, with advantages
in both of the remaining objectives, cost and client access. Montana now dominates Lombard (see "Eliminate Office Size; Select
Montana" table, page 94).

Alan signs the lease for space at Montana, confident that he
has thought through the decision carefully, considered every alternative and objective, and made the smart choice.

## Practical Advice for Making Even Swaps

Once you get the hang of it, the mechanical part of the even swap
method becomes easy—almost a game. Determining the relative
value of different consequences—the essence of any tradeoff
process—is the hard part. By design, the even swap method allows you to concentrate on the value determinations one at a
time, giving each careful thought. While there's no easy recipe
for deciding how much of one consequence to swap for some
amount of another (every swap requires subjective judgment),
you can help ensure that your tradeoffs are sound by keeping the
following suggestions in mind.

**Make the easier swaps first.** Determining the value of some
swaps will be more difficult for you than determining the value of
others. In choosing among airlines, for example, you may be able
to calculate, in fairly precise terms, the monetary value of a cer-

tain number of frequent flyer miles. After all, you know how many miles it would take to earn a free flight and what a flight would cost. Swapping between fares and miles will therefore be a straightforward process. On the other hand, swapping between airline safety records and flight departure times will be much less clear-cut. In this case, you should make the fare-mile swap—the easier swap—first. Often, you will be able to reach a decision (or at least eliminate a number of alternatives) by just making the easier swaps, saving you from having to wrestle with the harder ones at all.

**Concentrate on the amount of the swap, not on the perceived importance of the objective.** It doesn't make sense to say that one objective is more important than another without considering the degree of variation among the consequences for the alternatives under consideration. Is salary more important than vacation? It depends. If the salaries of all the alternative jobs are similar but their vacation times vary widely, then the vacation objective may be more important than the salary objective.

Concentrating on an objective's perceived importance can get in the way of making wise tradeoffs. Consider the debate that might occur in a town trying to decide whether public library hours should be cut to save money. The library advocate declares, "Preserving current library hours is much more important than cutting costs!" The fiscal watchdog counters, "No, we absolutely have to cut our budget deficit! Saving money is more important." Were the two sides to focus on the actual amounts of time and money in question, they might find it easy to reach agreement. If cutting branch hours by just two hours one morning a week saves $250,000 annually, the library advocate might agree that the harm to the library would be small compared to the amount saved, especially considering other possible uses for the money. If, instead, the savings were a mere $25,000 annually, even the fiscal watchdog might agree that harm to the library wouldn't be worth the savings. The point is this: when you make even swaps, concentrate not on the importance of the objectives but on the importance of the amounts in question.

**Value an incremental change based on what you start with.**   When you swap a piece of a larger whole—for example, a portion of an office's overall square footage—you need to think of its value in terms of the whole. For example, adding 300 square feet to a 700-square-foot office may make the difference between being cramped and being comfortable, whereas adding 300 square feet to a spacious 1,000-square-foot-office may not be nearly as valuable to you. The value of the 300 square feet, like the value of anything being swapped, is relative to what you start with. It's not enough to look just at the size of the slice; you also need to look at the size of the pie.

**Make consistent swaps.**   Although the value of what you swap is relative, the swaps themselves should be logically consistent. If you would swap A for B and B for C, you should be willing to swap A for C. Let's say you manage an environmental protection program charged with preserving wilderness quality and expanding salmon spawning habitats for as low a cost as possible. In a cost-benefit analysis, you might calculate that both one square mile of wilderness and two miles of river spawning habitat have values equivalent to $400,000. In making your swaps, you should therefore equate one square mile of wilderness with two miles of river spawning habitat. From time to time, check your swaps for consistency.

**Seek out information to make informed swaps.**     Swaps among consequences require judgments, but these judgments can be buttressed by facts and analysis. In making your environmental tradeoffs, for example, you might ask a fish biologist to provide information about how many salmon would use a mile of newly created spawning habitat, how many eggs might eventually hatch, how many fish would survive to swim downstream, and how many would return to spawn in the river years later. Whether a mile of spawning habitat would result in an increase in the annual salmon run of 20 or 2,000 adult salmon will likely make a big difference in the relative value you establish for that habitat.

For some decisions, you yourself will be the source of much of the relevant information. If you are trading off vacation time and salary in choosing among job offers, only you know how you would spend a two-week versus a four-week vacation and the value of the difference to you. You should be as rigorous in thinking through your own judgments as you are in assessing objective data from outside sources. No matter how subjective a tradeoff, you never want to be guided by whim—think carefully about the value of each consequence *to you*.

**Practice makes perfect.**     Like any new approach to an old problem, the even swap method will take some getting used to. The first few times you make swaps, you may struggle with the overall process as well as with each assessment of relative value. Fortunately, the process itself is relatively simple, and it always works the same way. Once you get the hang of it, you'll never have to think about it again. Deciding on appropriate swaps, on the other hand, will never be easy—each swap will require careful judgment. As you gain experience, though, you'll also gain understanding. You'll become more and more skilled at zeroing in on and expressing the real sources of value. You'll know what's important and what's not. Perhaps the greatest benefit of the even swap method is that it forces you to think through the value of every tradeoff in a rational, measured way. In the end, that's the secret of making smart choices.

## APPLICATION

### To Renovate or Move?

Still unsure of their decision after reviewing their consequences table, Drew and Darlene decide to try to rank the alternatives by objective. For each of their main objectives, they compare the houses in terms of the relevant subobjectives. Regarding house quality, they easily determine a ranking that places Amherst first, followed by Wade, Eaton, West Boulevard, and finally School Street. Although based on the information about house quality pulled together by Darlene, the ranking derives not from a formula but from judgments the couple made. Satisfied and encouraged by their first stab at rankings, they move on to the other objectives, drawing up the table on page 100 after much further thought and discussion.

Darlene begins drawing some conclusions. "These rankings make some things pretty clear. For instance, they confirm our earlier conclusion that Eaton should be eliminated—Wade is better on every main objective." It doesn't matter that Eaton is better than Wade on some subobjectives, as this is accounted for in the ranking on the main objectives.

Drew adds further assessments. "I think that West Boulevard could go, too. Wade is better on five main objectives and inferior by only a small difference in cost. In addition, look at West Boulevard and School Street. They are even on location: School Street is in a better neighborhood, but its schools are worse. West Boulevard beats School Street on house quality and yard, but School Street is slightly less expensive. All in all, School Street seems about equal to West Boulevard, so if West Boulevard goes, School Street should, too. Do you agree?"

"Yes, I do! So we're down to the crux: do we want to try for Wade or Amherst?"

"Daddy, I think we should move to Wade Street."

"Why do you think so?"

"Well, the scores on your table add up to 12 points for Wade and 15 for Amherst, and the fewer the points the better."

Drew and Darlene mull this over. Is it right to just add the ranking

### Ranking the Alternatives for Each Main Objective for the Mathers' New House

| Objectives | Amherst | Eaton | School | Wade | West Boulevard |
|---|---|---|---|---|---|
| **Good location** | 5 | 4 | 2 (tie) | 1 | 2 (tie) |
| **Quality of school** | 2 | 4 | 5 | 1 | 3 |
| **Quality of neighborhood** | 1 | 4 | 2 | 3 | 5 |
| **Quality of house** | 1 | 3 | 5 | 2 | 4 |
| Yard | 1 | 3 | 5 | 2 | 4 |
| Cost | 5 | 4 | 1 | 3 | 2 |

scores? No, they finally decide; both Wade and Amherst are better on three objectives. The rankings capture neither the degree of superiority of one over the other nor the nature of the differences, and both are important for their decision.

To better compare the pros and cons of Wade and Amherst, the Mathers return to the consequences table (page 76). After a while, Drew says, "I've been agonizing over this table, and it's hard to see which is better. One thing I realize now is that I don't really understand the cost implications of either alternative very well. Let me work on that for an hour or so."

Drew goes to work on the monthly costs of ownership. In other words, he digs deeper into the cost portion of the consequences table. He considers mortgage, upkeep, insurance, and real estate taxes. He reduces the mortgage interest and real estate taxes figures by the amount the Mathers would save in deductions on their income tax. He also estimates the equity buildup after 10 years resulting from the appreciation of each house and the paying down of the mortgages. After completing his financial analysis, he summarizes his conclusions to Darlene. "It all boils down to Amherst's being about $150 per month more expensive than Wade. However, that added expense per month buys us something financially. We'd have more equity building up at Amherst than at Wade—about $24,000 more in 10 years, I estimate. That has to be taken into account. These numbers surprise me. I thought that Amherst would be much more expensive than Wade, but it really isn't. With Amherst, we'd have a sort of forced savings plan."

"So are you tilting toward Amherst?"

"No, no, no. I'm just saying that as far as cost is concerned, it's not much of a difference. We have to look at all the other factors, too."

Darlene says, "I've been trying to think systematically about this. It seems to me that the choice boils down to this: Wade is way better on location, somewhat better on cost, slightly better on school quality, a little worse on neighborhood quality, a little worse on house quality, and not quite as good on yard quality."

"That's still apples and oranges—evaluations across categories. How can we compare less commuting time with better house quality?"

"Well, for me the answer seems clear now. And it was John who helped me decide. Do you want to know my reasoning, or do you want to struggle more yourself? I don't want to bias you."

"I'm all ears. How did John help? I suspect he prefers Wade because there are loads of kids on the block."

"When I considered the longer commuting time for Amherst, I had in mind your frustration and the time you'd waste stuck in traffic. But John had a different twist. He said, 'If Daddy has to travel more, he won't have time to play with me before dinner.' And this got me thinking about the real downside of a longer commute. As it is, you only have about two hours between the time you get home and the time John goes to bed. A longer commute will just cut into the time you have to spend with John and the baby. That's serious! So . . . I think the advantages in location for Wade outweigh its other slight deficiencies."

"Boy, am I glad you think so. I didn't want to make too much of more travel time, because it falls mostly on my shoulders, but I agree with John. I would miss not having time to play with him after work."

"And there's another reason I'd like you home earlier. You're sweeter when you're not frustrated with traffic."

So the Mathers call Anne and ask her to put in a bid of $190,000 for the Wade Street house. It is accepted the next day.

## Lessons from the Application

The Mathers organized their information wisely to help them evaluate their alternatives. The ranking on each main objective allowed them to see that the Eaton house was dominated and that West Boulevard and School Street were practically dominated. It then boiled down to a decision between Amherst and Wade. As is often the case, when it gets down to decision time, there was an aspect of consequences—in this case, cost—that needed further exploration before they were comfortable making a decision.

What would we have suggested the Mathers do to better appraise the suitability of the remaining two houses?

- In specifying their original objectives and subobjectives, the Mathers did not ask "Why?" often enough. Why, for example, did they want to reduce commute time? If they had, perhaps they would have identified earlier the objectives of increasing Drew's play time with John and reducing his grumpiness.
- The Mathers could have used the even swap method to compare the relative pros and cons of the final two contending houses. This would help identify the Wade house as the smart choice and clarify the basis for this choice.
- When only Amherst and Wade remained as contenders, the Mathers could have listed the pros and cons of one house versus the other and applied Benjamin Franklin's method for balancing the pros and cons to help make a choice.

After thinking very carefully about which house to try to buy, the Mathers spent too little time deciding how much to offer. Deciding on a bid is a separate decision from which house to purchase, and it's a decision worthy of careful thought. Maybe an offer of $172,000 would have been accepted, saving the Mathers $18,000. The decision of what to offer comes with significant uncertainties: Are there other bids from other potential buyers? What might they be? What offer will the seller accept? How might the seller counter? In the next chapter, we'll discuss how to systematically address such uncertainties to help make a smart choice.

# CHAPTER 7

# Uncertainty

In the preceding chapters, we've laid out a comprehensive approach to making smart choices when, for practical purposes, you can know the consequences of each alternative *before* deciding. We now turn to situations in which—no matter how much time and thought you expend—you won't know what the consequences will be until *after* deciding. They're uncertain. When you choose, you may know what *might* happen, but you won't know what *will* happen.

Because life is full of uncertainties, many of the decisions you make will involve calculated risks: investing in a mutual fund, accepting a blind date, deciding to have a child, asking for a raise or promotion, starting a business, launching a new product. You can't snap your fingers and make the uncertainties go away. But you can raise the odds of making a good decision in uncertain situations. How? The first step is to acknowledge the existence of the uncertainties. Then you need to think them through systematically, understanding the various outcomes that might unfold, their likelihoods, and their impacts.

# Distinguish Smart Choices from Good Consequences

Whenever uncertainty exists, there can be no guarantee that a smart choice will lead to good consequences. Although many people judge the quality of their own and others' decisions by the quality of the consequences—by how things turn out—this is an erroneous view, as these two examples illustrate:

**A smart choice, a bad consequence.**    Eager to build a long-delayed addition to his home in North Carolina, Lee Huang carefully weighs the risks and benefits of starting work in December. Construction in the region, with its usually mild winters and light snowfall, typically goes on year round, and the current long-range weather forecasts predict normal conditions. Because the chances of serious weather-related problems are small, Lee decides to proceed. The winter, however, turns out to be the worst in 40 years. The project takes an extra month and costs $6,000 more than planned. Was this a stupid choice? No! The choice was fine; only the consequence was bad. Lee might say, "If I had only known the weather would be so bad, I'd have waited until spring!" But how could he have known?

**A poor choice, a good consequence.**    Roberta Giles, an inexperienced investor, acts on a tip from an acquaintance and, without doing any research, invests in a venture to build a large apartment building. For the first few years after construction, the building reaches only 75 percent occupancy and runs deep in the red. But, just as bankruptcy seems inevitable, a large business unexpectedly moves into a nearby office park. Soon, the apartment building is full, with a waiting list for vacancies. Rents skyrocket. Three years later, Roberta sells out for four times her initial investment. Was the investment a smart choice? No! The decision making was terrible, even though the consequence was good. Would other decisions made the same way turn out as well? Extremely doubtful.

Decisions under uncertainty should be judged by the quality of the decision making, not by the quality of the consequences. Robert F. O'Keeffe, the retired head of claims for INA (now CIGNA), one of the largest U.S. property and casualty insurance companies, understands this distinction well (perhaps in part because he's an avid poker player). In a recent conversation, Bob stated his philosophy:

> If I try to settle a major liability claim out of court and the other side's final offer exceeds what my analysis shows to be a fair value, I take the case to trial. Often I either win outright, or the jury awards the plaintiff less than my calculated value or less than the plaintiff's final offer. But sometimes the jury award exceeds what I could have settled for. The difference can be tens of thousands of dollars or even hundreds of thousands. In these cases, was it a mistake to refuse the offer? No. I just remind myself that another jury who heard the same evidence might have made a more favorable award.

O'Keeffe's overall record attests to the quality of his decisions, yet over the course of his career he has encountered many surprises and upsets. The best that O'Keeffe or any of us can do in making an important decision is to ensure we use a sound process that enables us to identify and think clearly about uncertainty. We can't make uncertainty disappear, but we can address it explicitly in our decision-making process.

## Use Risk Profiles to Simplify Decisions Involving Uncertainty

Uncertainty adds a new layer of complexity to decision making. A single decision may involve many different uncertainties, of varying levels of importance, and they may all interact, in tangled ways, to determine the ultimate consequences. To make sense of uncertainty, you need to find a way to simplify it—to isolate its elements and evaluate them one by one. You can do this by using *risk profiles*.

A risk profile captures the essential information about the way uncertainty affects an alternative. It answers four key questions:

- What are the key *uncertainties*?
- What are the possible *outcomes* of these uncertainties?
- What are the *chances* of occurrence of each possible outcome?
- What are the *consequences* of each outcome?

By providing a consistent basis for comparing the uncertainties affecting each of your alternatives, risk profiles allow you to focus in on the key factors that should influence your choice, ignoring peripheral factors. Consider this simple example. Joe Lazzarino has kept his small consulting firm in business over the last five years by bidding on many small public and private engineering projects. His company consistently makes a modest profit, but

Joe's starting to get bored—he's eager for new and bigger challenges. One day, he receives word that a government agency has issued a request for proposals for a large, multiyear contract. Joe sees that winning the contract would provide enormous benefits, but the huge costs associated with preparing a proposal could deplete his firm's resources. And, of course, the agency's response to his proposal is uncertain. He might be granted a full contract, a partial contract, or no contract at all.

Joe creates a risk profile for the alternative of preparing and submitting a proposal. He succinctly describes the possible outcomes, their chances of occurring, and the associated consequences. He writes them up in a simple table, as shown below. Studying the risk profile, Joe sees a clear choice. Winning a partial contract (outcome $B$) or a full contract (outcome $C$) are much more likely outcomes than losing the bid altogether (outcome $A$), and both $B$ and $C$ would lead to consequences that are much more desirable than the current situation. Joe decides to go for it.

Joe's experience with bidding, together with the limited number of alternatives and possible outcomes, made it fairly easy for him to draw up the risk profile. Many decision problems involving uncertainty will present greater challenges. In all cases, though, the development of clear, thorough risk profiles is the all-important first step.

## How to Construct a Risk Profile

Now let's look at how you'd go about constructing a more complex risk profile. Janet Ellingwood, the owner of a mail order firm

## Joe's Risk Profile for Preparing and Submitting a Proposal

*Uncertainty: Government response to bid*

| Outcome | Chance | Consequences |
| --- | --- | --- |
| A. No contract | Least likely | Bad. Will need to reduce staff, borrow heavily, and scramble for some small contracts. |
| B. Partial contract | Most likely | Pretty good. More firm stability. Will make a decent profit. |
| C. Full contract | Somewhat likely | Wonderful. Not only very profitable, but also professionally interesting. Will greatly enhance our reputation. |

in Denver, is planning a summer party for her 55 employees. They've worked very hard over the past year, and she wants to use this party to recognize and celebrate their efforts. Her objectives for the party are fun, family involvement, and reasonable expense. She informally polls her employees and finds that they favor two alternatives: a picnic at a mountain retreat with a swimming pool and a ball field, or a dinner dance at a downtown hotel.

When Janet looks at her three objectives, the picnic seems the better choice: Everyone would enjoy the games and facilities, it would involve employees' kids, and the cost would be low. But the success of the picnic, much more than that of the hotel dance, would depend on the weather. While Janet knows that a sunny day would be more likely than a rainy one at that time of year, she also knows that Denver could experience one of its occasional summer downpours. If it did rain, the picnic would likely be a flop. Food could be served under a tent—for an added cost—but most other activities would be curtailed, and many people would stay home or leave early. On the other hand, few people would pass up the dance because of rain, and although the hotel's out-door patio—a memorable place on a nice evening—would be un-usable, the ballroom would still be elegant and spacious enough for a pleasant evening.

In thinking quickly through the two alternatives, Janet has al-ready roughly answered the four risk profile questions. She's identified the uncertainty (weather), the possible outcomes (rain or shine), their chances (rain less likely), and the consequences (picnic a flop in the rain). In some cases, such brief, informal de-scriptions may be adequate to make a final decision, but Janet doesn't feel that the information is sufficient to allow her to make a smart choice. She proceeds systematically to clarify the uncer-tainties, outcomes, chances, and consequences impinging on her decision.

**Identify the key uncertainties.**    Virtually any decision involves un-certainties, but most uncertainties don't influence consequences enough to matter. Selecting the uncertainties important enough to include in a risk profile requires just two steps:

- List all the uncertainties that might significantly influence the consequences of any alternatives.
- Consider these uncertainties one at a time and determine whether and to what degree their various possible outcomes might influence the decision. When there are

many possible uncertainties, winnow them down to the few
that are likely to matter most.

Janet's decision presents a number of uncertainties in addition
to the weather, including attendance and cost. In considering the
possible outcomes for attendance, Janet concludes that nearly all
employees would plan to attend either event and that knowing
the exact number wouldn't influence her choice. To evaluate
costs, Janet asks the events managers of the two sites for estimates.
She learns that the picnic would cost approximately $6,000 and
the dinner dance roughly $12,500. These estimates would vary
slightly depending on the exact number of guests and their food,
beverage, and entertainment choices, but the variation would not
significantly influence Janet's thinking. So, even though attendance and cost are subject to some uncertainty, the possible outcomes would not impact the ultimate consequences enough to
make a difference in Janet's choice.

That leaves weather as the key uncertainty. No matter how appealing the picnic, if it rains many people will not attend or will
leave early. The picnic would be a washout.

**Define outcomes.**   The possible outcomes of each uncertainty
must now be specified. This requires answering two questions:

- How many possible outcomes need to be defined to express the extent of each uncertainty?
- How can each outcome best be defined?

The number of outcomes you'll need to specify will depend on
the kind of uncertainty you're addressing. Some uncertainties in-
herently have a small number of clearly defined potential out-

comes: Which of the two contestants will win the chess match? Will the pending legislation pass or be voted down? Others entail a large number of potential outcomes: How many people will attend next Saturday's football game? How much money will I make or lose from buying this stock?

When there are many possible outcomes, you should simplify your expression of them by organizing them into ranges, or categories. The categories can be either quantitative ($10,000 to $20,000, $20,000 to $30,000, and so on) or descriptive (high, medium, low; successful, unsuccessful, neutral). In some cases, it may be helpful to assign a representative value to a numerical range—for example, using $25,000 as a stand-in for the range $20,000 to $30,000—to make calculations and comparisons easier.

Because complexity increases as the number of categories increases, you should always seek to narrow the set of outcomes down to the fewest possible—enough to fully describe the uncertainty, but no more. Start by defining a small number of outcomes, and then add more only as needed. If you're projecting the possible outcomes of a new product launch, for instance, you might start with just two categories: "High sales" and "Low sales." If they are insufficient to capture the range of outcomes, you would then create a new category, "Medium sales," containing part of what was previously in both the high and the low categories.

However many outcomes are designated, they must meet three further criteria. First, the categories must differ clearly from one another, with no overlaps (that is, they must be *mutually exclusive*). "Widely scattered showers" shouldn't be included in both "Rain" and "Shine." Second, the outcomes must include all possibilities, with every possible contingency falling within one or another cat-

egory (that is, they must be *collectively exhaustive*). "Widely scattered showers" must be included in either "Rain" or "Shine."
Third, the outcomes must be unambiguously defined, so that
when the uncertainty is resolved, the event can be clearly recognized as falling within one or another of the defined categories.
If widely scattered showers occurred, was the weather rain or
shine?

**Assign chances.**   Clearly defining the possible outcomes or categories of outcomes will help you in judging the chance, or likelihood, that each outcome will occur. Still, though, assigning
chances can be one of the toughest and most nerve-wracking
tasks in decision making, especially when you don't know very
much about the subject or when you're under time pressure. But
you can help ensure that your assessments are both reasonable
and useful by following these suggestions:

- **Use your judgment.**   Often, you can make a reasonable
  assessment of the chances of a given outcome based on
  your own knowledge and experience. Oddsmakers do it all
  the time in sports betting. Friends do it when they arrange
  blind dates. We all do it almost unconsciously in daily life:
  What are the chances I'll encounter delays on my home-
  ward commute this Friday?

- **Consult existing information.**   There will often be information available that will help you assign chances to outcomes. You should carefully consider all the potential
  sources of information—libraries, the Internet, documents
  in your organization, research data, professional publica-
  tions—that might shed light on the potential outcomes.
  Janet, for example, might get climatological data from the

weather bureau to help her assess whether it will rain on a summer afternoon or evening.

- **Collect new data.**   Sometimes the particular data you need may not be available off the shelf—you may need to collect them yourself. A food company might estimate the percentage of families who will buy a new brand of coffee by conducting a market trial or a telephone survey.

- **Ask experts.**   For most uncertainties, there will probably be someone out there who knows more about it than you do. Seek out an expert—your doctor, lawyer, or accountant, an economist—and elicit his or her judgment. In Janet's case, a local meteorologist would be an appropriate expert.

- **Break uncertainties into their components.**   Sometimes dividing an uncertainty into its components, thinking about the components, and then combining the results will help in establishing probabilities. An entrepreneur recognizes that the success of a new car wash in an area currently undergoing development will depend on the relative number of cars brought to the area by the different proposals for the adjoining site: a shopping mall or an office park. He can assign chances to various ranges of washes per day assuming the mall is built, and do likewise assuming the office park is constructed. He can then blend the results in proportion to the chances he assigns to the construction of a mall and of offices, to get an overall assessment of washes per day.

When expressing chances, qualitative terms may come first to mind. In casual conversation, people often describe chances using phrases such as "unlikely," "toss-up," "barely possible," "fairly likely," "pretty good chance," "almost sure," and so on. They do this not only because it's easy, but also because they think they're really communicating their judgments about likelihood. But one person's "fairly likely" may or may not be the same as the next person's. Such subjective phrases may be sufficient for personal decisions that will not need to be justified to others, but they're not precise enough for most decisions. In most cases, therefore, you will want to express chances quantitatively, as actual probabilities, using either a decimal (0.2) or a percentage (20 percent). Using numbers reduces the likelihood of miscommunication and sharpens decisions.

If you are having trouble expressing your judgment quantitatively, or getting someone else to do so, zero in from the extremes. If you ask the hostess at a busy, no-reservations restaurant the chances of getting seated at 5:30 P.M. on Thursday, she might respond, "I haven't a clue; either you will or you won't." (Ah, frustration!) Countering with the question, "Is the chance better than 25 percent?" will very often elicit something more useful: "Oh, much more than that." "More than 50 percent?" "Yes." "As much as 90 percent?" "Too high." The range has been narrowed to between 50 percent and 90 percent; a few more questions might provide an even more precise range.

Pinpoint precision usually isn't required in assigning chances. Frequently, knowing that a chance falls within a certain range is sufficient for guiding a decision. (See "Which Flight?" below.) If the estimated chance of some outcome falls between 30 percent and 50 percent, for example, compare the alternatives using 40 percent. Then reconsider them using 30 percent or 50 percent. More often than not, the change won't matter; the decision will remain the same.

However they are expressed, the probabilities for the outcomes of an uncertainty should always add up to 100 percent (or, if you express them as decimals, to 1.0). If the two categories for weather are "Rain" and "Shine" and if the probability of rain is 35 percent, then the probability of shine necessarily is 65 percent. Also remember that your assessment of the chances of an outcome occurring may change as circumstances change or as new information becomes available. As you proceed through your decision process, regularly reexamine the chances you've assigned to ensure their reasonableness based on your current information.

---

### Resolving a Decision with an Estimate of Uncertainty: Which Flight?

Mark Hata has a dilemma. Months ago, he arranged to take his 62-year-old mother on a week-long trip to London in October. Mark lives in Phoenix, his mother in Pittsburgh. They plan to meet at Dulles Airport in Washington, D.C., on a Saturday evening in time for a leisurely dinner, before taking the 10:00 P.M. flight to London.

But Mark has just learned that his daughter's soccer team has earned a spot in the league championship game, which is scheduled for 9:00 A.M. that same Saturday, and he would really love to attend. What to do?

Mark sees three alternatives:

1. Attend the game and reschedule his departure to London for Sunday, cutting a day off the trip. (Reticketing would cost $400, but plenty of seats are available.)
2. Stick with the original plan and miss the soccer game.
3. Attend the game and take a later flight to Dulles. If this flight is on time or no more than 30 minutes late, Mark will just have time to meet his

mother and make the flight to London. That nixes dinner but otherwise leaves their plan intact.

After some soul-searching, Mark decides he'd rather miss the game than shorten his mom's London vacation. But should he attend the game and gamble on getting to Washington on time? After more thought, he decides he'd take the chance if the risk of missing the London flight is less than 15 percent.

With his decision boiled down to assessing the probability that he will arrive at Dulles no more than 30 minutes late, Mark checks with his travel agent and learns that Dulles has an 80 percent on-time arrival record, with "on-time" defined as arriving within 15 minutes of the scheduled time. After asking a few more questions of the agent, Mark figures his odds of arriving within 30 minutes are much better than 80 percent, for three reasons. First, many late flights arrive within 30 minutes of the scheduled time. Second, Saturday flights encounter fewer air traffic delays than do weekday flights. And, third, Phoenix has few weather-related departure delays. He concludes that he has at least a 90 percent chance of making the London flight. His choice is now easy, though still worrisome. He attends his daughter's game—a 2-2 tie, cochampions— and arrives in Washington 15 minutes early. Not only did Mark make a smart choice, he enjoyed a good consequence.

---

**Clarify the consequences.**   Different outcomes will have different consequences, and these, too, must be defined. In general, you should follow the same process for defining consequences as we laid out in Chapter 5, expressing them as precisely as necessary to make an informed choice. Depending on the complexity of the decision, you should lay out the consequences in one of three ways:

- **A written description.**   Although the least precise, a broad written description may occasionally be good enough. But remember that, whereas phrases such as "marginal," "OK," or "a waste of effort with little to show" may suit personal decisions, they require too much interpretation to be readily communicable to others.

- **A qualitative description by objective.**   Consequences expressed qualitatively by objective include more information than simple written descriptions, as they break a consequence into its constituent parts. For an outdoor picnic, the consequences of sunny weather for each of Janet's objectives would be described as (1) high on fun, (2) high on family involvement, and (3) low on cost.

- **A quantitative description by objective.**   Though they may require the most time to develop, consequences expressed quantitatively by objective—such as cost estimates in dollars—are the clearest, the most easily comparable, and the easiest to use. The cost of a used car listed as "$5,000 plus or minus 10 percent" is more useful and meaningful than one listed as "low."

In all cases, though, keep in mind that descriptions of consequences need only be precise enough to provide the information needed to reach a smart choice. If your choice is clear with a written description, there's no need to spend the time to develop precise, quantitative estimates.

## Picture Risk Profiles with Decision Trees

Often, the development of risk profiles can itself clarify uncertainty to the point where the smart choice becomes obvious. But

## Decision Tree for Janet's Employee Party

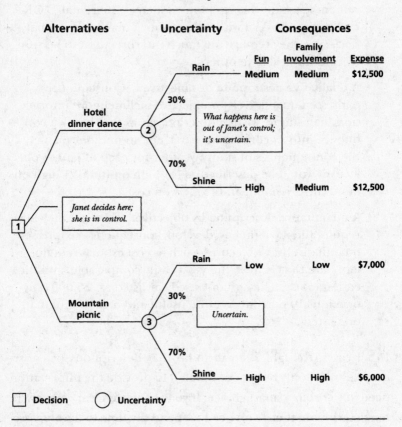

| Alternatives | Uncertainty | Consequences |

| | | Fun | Family Involvement | Expense |

Rain — Medium, Medium, $12,500

30%

Hotel dinner dance — 2

*What happens here is out of Janet's control; it's uncertain.*

70%

Shine — High, Medium, $12,500

*Janet decides here; she is in control.*

1

Rain — Low, Low, $7,000

30%

Mountain picnic — 3

*Uncertain.*

70%

Shine — High, High, $6,000

☐ Decision     ◯ Uncertainty

not always. Some decisions, particularly highly complex ones, will require further analysis. That's when a *decision tree* can be extremely useful. A decision tree provides a graphical representation—a picture—of the essence of a decision, displaying all the interrelationships among choices and uncertainties. In one sense, a decision tree is like a blueprint—it lays out, methodically and objectively, the architecture of a decision. And just as a builder would not set out to construct a house without a blueprint, a decision maker will often require a decision tree to resolve a tough choice under uncertain conditions.

The essence of Janet Ellingwood's employee party problem, for example, can be plotted in a decision tree, as we see on page 120. The tree begins at the point of the decision (the square labeled 1), with the initial branches representing the competing alternatives. In Janet's case, there are two alternatives, hotel dinner dance and mountain picnic, so there are two branches. Each alternative branch leads to a fork (the circles labeled 2 and 3), indicating an uncertainty. Each possible outcome of the uncertainty—in this case, rain or shine—is represented by a branch leading out from the fork. These outcome branches are labeled with their respective chance of occurring. (Janet uses 30 percent for the chance of rain, a judgment she elicited from a local meteorologist.) Each of the outcome branches in turn leads to different consequences, which are summarized, by objective, at the tips of the tree.

This simple decision tree, with its four possible paths, shows how pictures can clarify the relationships among alternatives, uncertainties, and consequences. It brings risk profiles to life. Seeing her decision presented this way immediately sharpens Janet's thinking. She concludes that a successful picnic would meet her objectives so much better than would the dinner dance that it is worth taking a 30 percent chance on rain. She opts for the picnic.

Decision trees are especially useful for explaining decision processes to others. (Hence the careful numbering of the branching points and the labeling of the branches.) Getting into the habit of sketching decision trees, even for relatively simple decisions involving uncertainty, can enhance your decision-making skills in two ways. First, decision trees encourage thorough, logical thinking about a problem—a useful habit to cultivate. Second, mastering the mechanical skill of tree construction on simple problems will make it easier to use the technique for more complex ones, such as the one illustrated in the following application.

## APPLICATION

### To Settle or Not to Settle?

Karen Plavonic hasn't had a good night's sleep in weeks. Her stomach is always in knots. Day and night she anguishes over whether to accept a $300,000 offer to settle her personal injury lawsuit. On the one hand, she knows there's a good chance of getting much more—maybe as much as a million dollars—if she refuses and goes to trial. But, on the other hand, she could lose in court and end up with nothing. Then she'd wish she had accepted the offer (and she knows her mother would never let her forget her mistake!).

Karen, 27 years old and single, feels she may have contributed in a small way to the automobile accident that has left her slightly disabled, disfigured, and plagued with mounting medical expenses. Though she doesn't want to look foolish for "throwing away" the settlement, her lawyer, Sam Barnes, is pressuring her in the opposite direction. He is urging her not to weaken, not to let the other guy off the hook. Karen, however, can't overcome residual feelings of guilt about the accident, despite her relative innocence and the greater harm she has suffered—facial scars, impaired mobility in her neck and left shoulder, and loss of income. She feels keenly the possibility that she might break down in court, jeopardizing her case. Every friend, relative, coworker, and acquaintance she's ever had is giving her conflicting advice about what to do. She just can't decide.

## Karen's Decision Problem

Karen's close friend Jane Stewart has suffered with her through the aftermath of the accident, and she is now serving as Karen's sounding board for her soul-wrenching inner debate about the lawsuit. Jane, a management consultant with professional experience in facilitating decision making, has undertaken to help Karen think through her situation systematically, to end her emotionally devastating indecision. Jane wants to help Karen decide whether she should go to court or settle out of court and to feel comfortable that she is making an appropriate decision. As she tells Karen, who hopes her luck will finally turn, "Most of the time luck favors the better decision maker."

Together, Karen and Jane isolate three essential considerations on which Karen's decision will hinge:

1. The chance of winning the trial and, if won, the chances of different possible jury awards.
2. The time and psychological stresses associated with going to trial and of not going to trial, together with the degree of Karen's regret if she loses or elation if she wins.
3. Karen's willingness to take risk.

In addition to going to court or settling for $300,000, Karen and Jane recognize a third alternative: waiting for a better settlement offer. Based on his knowledge of the opposing lawyer, Sam doesn't think another offer will be forthcoming. But Karen and Jane decide that, if Karen chooses to settle, she should keep her options open until the last minute.

To complete her risk profile of the go-to-court alternative, Karen will need to hear Sam's judgment about the chance of a positive trial outcome and of different award amounts. Karen schedules a meeting with him and Jane, for which Jane prepares some materials.

## Karen's Decision Tree

At their meeting, Jane passes around a diagram (below) that describes Karen's decision problem as a decision tree. Reading from the left, the box labeled 1 represents Karen's basic decision: go to court or settle out of court. Deciding to settle, the lower branch, entails no uncertainty. But the decision to go to court, the upper branch, leads to two uncertainties: Will Karen win or lose (fork 2), and if she wins, how much will she get (fork 3)?

The range of figures off fork 3, from $200,000 to $1,000,000, represents the possible jury awards, which Jane derived from Karen's earlier discussions with Sam. The figure $210,000 at the end of the settlement branch represents what Karen would have left after paying Sam his 30

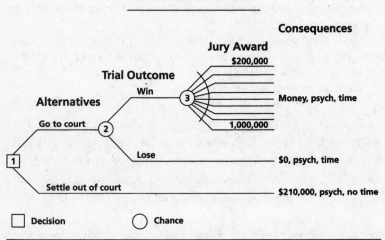

**Karen's Decision Tree**

Consequences

Jury Award
$200,000

Trial Outcome
Win

Alternatives

Money, psych, time

Go to court   2

3

1,000,000

1

Lose

$0, psych, time

Settle out of court

$210,000, psych, no time

☐ Decision            ◯ Chance

percent fee. In addition to money, the tree notes two other possible consequences: "psych" indicates that the outcome might exact non-monetary costs, including sleeplessness, anxiety, and regret, and "time" indicates that the outcome would entail a further investment of time.

## Karen's Chances

Karen and Jane now call on Sam's expertise to quantify the likelihood that Karen will win the trial. Sam has told Karen that she has a "pretty good" chance of winning, based on the outcomes of similar cases, the record of the judge, and his assessment of his own litigation skills.

Jane probes the meaning of "pretty good," trying to arrive at a hard number, which would sharpen the analysis. She asks Sam, "How would you translate 'pretty good' into a probability?"

"I just don't think that way," Sam answers. "I don't see how you can put a number on everything, especially things as subjective as winning a trial."

Jane turns to Karen. "How do you interpret that, Karen? Give me some number."

"Oh, I'd say that Sam thinks our chance of winning is around 20 or 30 percent."

Sam protests. "That's not what I said! When I say a pretty good chance, I mean something more than that!"

"How much more? More than 50-50?"

"Certainly. More than 50 percent."

"How much more?"

"Oh, I don't know that you can put a precise number on it. It certainly isn't as high as 90 percent. In jury trials you can never be that sure. It's maybe somewhere between 60 and 80 percent."

"Would you say that 70 percent is reasonable, or high, or low?"

"It's a good estimate, as close as we can get."

"OK, let's talk about the uncertainties of the jury award at fork 3."

Jane probes Sam's knowledge about the possible jury award. After an

## Chances for the Jury Award
## if Karen Wins

| Interval of Jury Award | Outcome | Chance | Representative Amount |
|---|---|---|---|
| From $200,000 to $410,000 | Low | 25% | $300,000 |
| From $410,000 to $550,000 | Medium | 25 | 470,000 |
| From $550,000 to $700,000 | High | 25 | 610,000 |
| From $700,000 to $1,000,000 | Very High | 25 | 800,000 |

hour or so of give and take, she prepares a table (above) summarizing his judgments. It divides the previously determined $800,000 range ($200,000 to $1 million) into four equally likely outcome intervals, labeled "Low," "Medium," "High," and "Very high." A representative amount for each interval, also listed in the table, makes it easier to interpret the implications of the jury award uncertainty. The figure $300,000, for example, stands for the range $200,000 to $410,000.

## Karen's Consequences

The task now is to factor in the nonmonetary costs to Karen of pursuing a jury trial: her time, her anxieties about losing, her lingering guilt about her role in the accident, her apprehension of the criticism of others (especially her mother) if she does lose after turning down a sure thing, and her own potential regrets on the same score.

Karen and Jane use the even swap method (as described in Chapter 6) to assign monetary values to the intangible costs. As shown in the "Adjustments" column for summarizing Karen's consequences (page 127), they use negative dollar amounts to represent what Karen would sacrifice, or "pay," to rid herself of all time and psychological impacts, and positive dollar amounts to represent the equivalent value she would gain, or "earn," from her elation at winning a very high award. The

## Net Equivalent Dollar Consequences for Karen

| Outcome | Gross Amount | Deduction of Attorney's Fees (30%) | Adjustments for Time and Psychological Impacts | Equivalent Monetary Amount |
|---|---|---|---|---|
| **WIN** | | | | |
| Low | $300,000 | − $ 90,000 | − $25,000 | $185,000 |
| Medium | 470,000 | − 141,000 | − 19,000 | 310,000 |
| High | 610,000 | − 183,000 | − 12,000 | 415,000 |
| Very high | 800,000 | − 240,000 | 20,000 | 580,000 |
| **LOSE** | 0 | 0 | − 30,000 | − 30,000 |
| **SETTLE** | 300,000 | − 90,000 | 0 | 210,000 |

## Karen's Decision Tree with Consequences and Probabilities Added

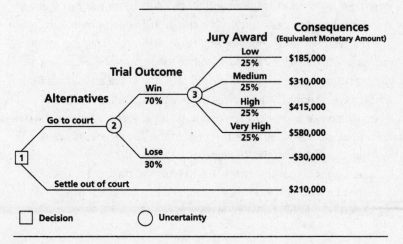

□ Decision          ◯ Uncertainty

## Karen's Risk Profile for
## Going to Court

---

*Uncertainty: Trial outcome and jury award*

| Outcome | Chance | Consequences (Equivalent Monetary Amount) |
|---|---|---|
| **LOSE** | 30.0% | − $ 30,000 |
| **WIN** | | |
| Low award | 17.5 | $   185,000 |
| Medium award | 17.5 | 310,000 |
| High award | 17.5 | 415,000 |
| Very high award | 17.5 | 580,000 |
| | 100% | |

adjustment figures vary with the amount of the award, reflecting different balances of anxiety to satisfaction or regret to elation.

Once they have established equivalent monetary values of the intangible costs, Karen and Jane can add those values to (or subtract them
from) the award amount to calculate the overall value of each outcome.
The numbers in the column labeled "Equivalent Monetary Amount" thus
represent the net values to Karen from the representative awards, after
deducting her lawyer's fees (30%) and factoring in the adjustment
amounts. Jane adds the net values as well as the chances to Karen's
decision tree (see page 127). She also summarizes them in a risk profile (see
above), where the 17.5 percents represent the 70 percent chance of
winning the trial times the 25 percent of each award.

Karen sighs. "You sure have clarified what's at stake in my decision,
Jane. But I still don't know what I should do. Should I take the
$300,000? Or should I take my chance in court?"

"Well," Jane responds, "that depends on how you feel about taking risks. That's the final piece of the puzzle."

(*To be continued in Chapter 8.*)

## Lessons from the Application

Thanks in large part to Jane's guidance and Sam's input, Karen now has excellent risk profiles for her two alternatives: to settle or to go to court. Her case illustrates four essential points to keep in mind when describing and comparing risk profiles.

- Strive to use numbers to clarify the chances of different outcomes. People sometimes take refuge in vague qualitative descriptions of chances in order to avoid commitment, responsibility, or second-guessing. They may have to be pressed hard to quantify their judgments, but as Karen's case demonstrates, the greater precision and usefulness of numbers makes it worth the effort needed to get them.
- Clarify the consequences by being specific. By dividing the broad span between $200,000 and $1,000,000 into four narrower, equally likely ranges, with a representative dollar amount for each, Karen gained a much better appreciation for what winning might mean to her.
- Use the even swap method to convert intangible concerns into a meaningful equivalent value. This process improved Karen's understanding of the possible consequences of her choices, because it helped her to think hard about how much she valued the "intangibles." She could then combine this with any dollar award she might receive, subtract attorney's fees, and arrive at a single indicator of the net equivalent dollar amount for that consequence.
- Take time to think about the important uncertainties influencing a decision. Constructing risk profiles does not require much time or effort or any specialized knowledge. It does require an honest effort to identify the key uncertainties and their possible outcomes and to clarify the chances and consequences of each.

# CHAPTER 8

# Risk Tolerance

A PERSON'S ATTITUDE TOWARD RISK is as individual as his or her personality. Some people avoid risk at all costs—they put all their retirement savings into certificates of deposit insured by the federal government. Others embrace risk—they invest all their money in options, in penny stocks, in junk bonds. Most of us fall somewhere in between. We take on some degree of risk, knowing that it goes hand in hand with reward, but not so much that we can't sleep at night.

How can you take your personal tolerance for risk into account in making decisions? We saw in the last chapter that choosing under uncertainty boils down to choosing among the risk profiles of your various alternatives. Once you've specified the risk profiles, you can compare them and readily eliminate all the poor choices. Often, the best choice will be obvious. But suppose you've done this and you still can't make up your mind. At this point, you need to focus not just on the risk profile, but on the degree of risk you are willing to assume.

Consider, for example, the following dilemma. Years ago, Robert

Goldman, now 68, lost the vision in his left eye. His vision in his right eye has deteriorated in recent years due to a cataract. Now, even with his glasses, his corrected vision is only about 20/50, and anything he looks at is fuzzy, particularly at night. As a result, he has been advised to stop driving his car after dark.

Recently, Rob had his eyes examined, and his doctor, Joyce-lynn Eddy, raised the possibility of cataract surgery. For his particular case, the chances are 90 percent that cataract surgery would be successful, "success" meaning that his vision would be restored to 20/30, corrected, with no fuzziness. An unsuccessful outcome, which Dr. Eddy estimates as having a 10 percent likelihood, would erode his vision to no better than 20/100, corrected, with persisting fuzziness.

Rob quickly draws a decision tree (below), documenting the two alternatives (surgery or no surgery) and the two possible outcomes (successful or unsuccessful). The consequences of each

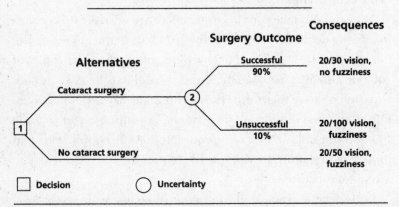

**Rob's Cataract Surgery Decision Tree**

outcome are described in terms of two fundamental objectives: acuity and clarity.

The tree clearly shows the risk profiles of the choices, yet Rob finds that the decision remains quite difficult. He would love to eliminate the fuzziness and once again have near-normal vision—and the chances of this are very good. But if the surgery failed, Rob would be worse off than he is now. He would have to quit driving altogether, give up some of his everyday physical activities, and curtail his reading or invest in expensive enlargers and other aids.

The essence of Rob's decision is that the surgery alternative offers him a 90 percent chance of restoring his vision, but a 10 percent chance of permanently worsening it. Clear enough? Yes. And yet so difficult. Should he take his chances on the surgery or play it safe with the status quo?

What would you decide? The smart choice for one person may not be the smart choice for another. You might decide not to have the surgery, but your next-door neighbor might opt for it. It all depends on one's attitude toward risk.

## Understand Your Willingness to Take Risks

Your risk tolerance expresses your willingness to take risk in your quest for better consequences—in Rob's case, better vision. It depends primarily on how significant you consider the downside—the poorer consequences of any decision—compared to the upside. If, like most people, you are risk averse, the poorer consequences will weigh more heavily in your mind than the better ones. The more heavily they weigh, the more risk averse you are.

Thus, to reflect your risk tolerance in a decision you need to think carefully about how desirable you consider the possible consequences relative to one another.

To see this, consider how two people, one moderately risk averse (Ms. Wary) and one very risk averse (Mr. Cautious), would evaluate a simple risky choice. Both are offered the opportunity to accept or reject a 50-50 chance of either making $10,000 or losing $5,000. A coin will be flipped. If it lands heads, they will receive $10,000 in cash. If it lands tails, they will lose $5,000.

How should they decide? They must weigh the chances of the upside and the downside and the desirability of each. In this case, because the upside and the downside are equally likely, the decision should hinge on how desirable they believe the upside is relative to the downside.

Mr. Cautious is very concerned about the impact of losing, fearing he'd have to borrow money or forgo important purchases to pay the penalty. He decides that the good fortune of receiving $10,000 doesn't compensate for the equally likely $5,000 loss. Ms. Wary would also hate to lose $5,000, knowing it would mean delaying her long-cherished plans to remodel her condo, but she likes the potential offered by a $10,000 windfall. With the extra cash, she could take her remodeling to the next level. The upside is desirable enough that she is willing to take the risk.

The same logic applies to all risk profiles, not just this simple one with two outcomes and consequences described in terms of a single objective, money. The basic principle is this: *the more desirable the better consequences of a risk profile relative to the poorer consequences, the more willing you will be to take the risks necessary to get them.*

But making the smart choice also requires balancing the desirabilities of the possible consequences with the probabilities that they will occur. If the chances in the decision above were changed to 90 percent in favor of gaining $10,000, even Mr. Cautious might be tempted. The downside remains just as undesirable relative to the upside, but because it is now much less likely, the improved chance of success will, for many people, more than compensate for the imbalance in desirability.

Once again, this logic applies to all risk profiles. *The more likely the outcomes with better consequences and the less likely the outcomes with poorer consequences, the more desirable the risk profile to you.*

## Incorporate Your Risk Tolerance into Your Decisions

To take your risk tolerance into account in comparing risk profiles, follow three simple steps:

- First, think hard about the relative desirability of the consequences of the alternatives you're considering.
- Second, balance the desirability of the consequences with their chances of occurring.
- Third, choose the most attractive alternative.

Taking these three steps enables Rob Goldman to reach a final decision about cataract surgery:

1. **Think hard about the desirabilities of the consequences.**
   Rob believes that restoring 20/30 vision without fuzziness would make a huge difference to him. He could resume driving at night, and tennis and traveling—two of his favorite pastimes—would become much easier. And although dropping to 20/100 would be bad—no question about it—he feels he has already made so many adjust-

ments to weakened vision that it wouldn't be the end of the world. He therefore decides that, in terms of desirability, the negative consequence of deteriorated vision only slightly outweighs the positive consequence of improved vision.

2. **Weight desirabilities by chances.**   More fully stated: weight the desirabilities of the consequences by the chances of their associated outcomes. If the odds of success were only 50-50, Rob wouldn't undergo the surgery. But the odds aren't even. Rob concludes that the fact that the upside is nine times more likely than the downside more than compensates for the fact that the undesirability of failure slightly outweighs the desirability of success.

3. **Compare and choose.**   When Rob now compares the surgery risk profile with the no-surgery alternative, his choice becomes abundantly clear: he calls Dr. Eddy's office to schedule the surgery.

## Quantify Risk Tolerance with Desirability Scoring

Suppose that, after having developed risk profiles and thought hard about the desirabilities of the consequences and the probabilities of the outcomes, you still can't decide. At this point, you need to be more precise about the relative desirability of each consequence. You need to move from a qualitative analysis, like Rob Goldman's, to a quantitative analysis. You follow the same general steps Rob did—determining desirabilities, weighting desirabilities by chances, comparing and choosing—but you use numbers to express the desirability of each consequence and, in turn, each alternative. Let's walk through the process.

1. **Assign desirability scores to all consequences.**   You begin by comparing the consequences and ranking them from best to worst. You assign the score of 100 to the best and 0 to the worst consequence. Then you assign a score to each of the remaining consequences that reflects its relative desirability. If, for example, you conclude that the desirability of a consequence is exactly halfway between that of the best and worst consequences, you'd assign it a score of 50. Check to be sure that all your scores are consistent, and adjust them as needed to reflect your true feelings about their respective consequences.

2. **Calculate each consequence's contribution to the overall desirability of the alternative.**   Outcomes with a low chance of occurring should have less influence on an alternative's overall desirability than outcomes with a high chance of occurring. Hence, you need to account for each outcome's chance of occurring—its probability. Now, to determine a consequence's contribution to the alternative's desirability, multiply its associated outcome's probability by its desirability score assigned in the first step. If your best consequence (desirability score of 100) had an outcome probability of 30 percent (0.3), its contribution would be 30 (i.e., $100 \times 0.3 = 30$). When an alternative results in a sure thing, its outcome has a probability of 1.0, and the contribution of its consequence will equal its desirability score.

3. **Calculate each alternative's overall desirability score.**   Now, add the individual consequence contributions to arrive at an overall desirability score for each alternative.

(Note that the overall desirability score of an alternative is the average of the desirability scores of its consequences, weighted by the chances of their associated outcomes.)

4. **Compare the overall desirability scores associated with the alternatives and choose.**   Now you have a solid, quantified basis for making a decision. Compare the overall desirability scores of each alternative, and choose the alternative with the highest score.

## Use Desirability Scoring to Make a Tough Decision

Going through the process of assigning desirability scores to consequences and calculating overall desirability scores for alternatives won't be necessary for most decisions. But for resolving some of life's most important and most complex decisions, it can be invaluable. Consider the situation facing Marisa Reyes, a graduate student in business administration who must decide within a matter of days between two attractive job offers, each involving a major uncertainty. One job is with the global accounting firm where Marisa worked for three years before leaving for graduate school. The other is with an international management consulting firm.

The career prospects and financial rewards at both firms are essentially equivalent. Marisa's decision therefore hinges on the nature and location of her initial job assignment. She has identified a number of objectives relating to the job assignment: good living conditions, including cultural and social attractions, quality housing, and interesting places to vacation; a challenging job with substantial responsibilities; and an opportunity to contribute to society by helping people.

The actual assignment she'll receive, however, is uncertain. Because she won't start for six months, neither of the companies will commit beforehand to a specific assignment, but each has narrowed the possible postings down to two. The consulting firm might initially post her to London—her dream—but it might also post her to Buenos Aires. The accounting firm would start her either in New York or in Santiago. Each alternative, in other words, leads to an uncertainty with two possible outcomes.

### Risk Profiles for
### Marisa's Job Decision

---

**ALTERNATIVE: ACCOUNTING FIRM**

**Uncertainty: Office Assignment**

| Outcome | Chance | Consequences | | |
| --- | --- | --- | --- | --- |
| | | *Living* | *Job* | *Society* |
| New York | 90% | Very good | Excellent | Fair |
| Santiago | 10 | Poor | Fair | Excellent |
| | 100% | | | |

**ALTERNATIVE: CONSULTING FIRM**

**Uncertainty: Office Assignment**

| Outcome | Chance | Consequences | | |
| --- | --- | --- | --- | --- |
| | | *Living* | *Job* | *Society* |
| Buenos Aires | 75% | Good | Good | Very good |
| London | 25 | Excellent | Excellent | Good |
| | 100% | | | |

Marisa carefully evaluates the possible assignments at each firm, and using the techniques outlined in Chapter 7, she creates the risk profiles shown on page 139. To judge the chances of each job posting, she talks in depth with the manager of human resources at each firm.

Marisa is unable to decide by simply comparing the risk profiles. The qualitative descriptions don't provide her with enough information. Therefore, she decides to compare the choices quantitatively. Before assigning desirability scores, she ranks the four possible consequences from best to worst, a good practice. As shown in the table below, she ranks the consequences associated with London first, New York second, Buenos Aires third, and Santiago last. She assigns a desirability score of 100 to the London consequences and 0 to the Santiago consequences, the best and worst of the locations. She then assigns to the Buenos Aires consequences a score of 50, judging its desirability to be halfway between that of Santiago and that of London. She then decides that the desir-

## Ranking and Scoring the Consequences of Marisa's Job Decision

| | | Consequences | | | | |
|---|---|---|---|---|---|---|
| Alternative | Outcome | *Living* | *Job* | *Society* | *Rank* | *Desirability Score* |
| **Consulting firm** | London | Excellent | Excellent | Good | 1 | 100 |
| **Accounting firm** | New York | Very good | Excellent | Fair | 2 | 80 |
| **Consulting firm** | Buenos Aires | Good | Good | Very good | 3 | 50 |
| **Accounting firm** | Santiago | Poor | Fair | Excellent | 4 | 0 |

# Determining the Overall Desirability for Marisa's Risk Profiles

*Accounting Firm*

| Outcome | Chance | Desirability Score | Contribution to Overall Desirability |
|---------|--------|--------------------|--------------------------------------|
| New York | 90% | 80 | 72 |
| Santiago | 10 | 0 | 0 |
| | 100% | | |
| | | Alternative's overall desirability score: | 72 |

*Consulting Firm*

| Outcome | Chance | Desirability Score | Contribution to Overall Desirability |
|---------|--------|--------------------|--------------------------------------|
| Buenos Aires | 75% | 50 | 37.5 |
| London | 25 | 100 | 25.0 |
| | 100% | | |
| | | Alternative's overall desirability score: | 62.5 |

ability of New York's consequences lies 60 percent of the way from the Buenos Aires consequences to London's, and so she assigns a score of 80 (80 is 60 percent of the way between 50 and 100). As a consistency check, Marisa asks herself whether all four of the scores reflect her true feelings, and she decides that they do.

Marisa then calculates the overall desirability score for the alternatives. She first multiplies the desirability score of each of the consequences by its associated outcome probability, which yields its contribution, as shown in the table above. She then adds the contributions of New York (72) and Santiago (0) to arrive at an overall desirability score for the accounting firm (72). Likewise, she adds the contributions of Buenos Aires (37.5) and London (25.0) to calculate the overall desirability score for the consulting firm (62.5). Relying on her calculations and the careful thought that preceded them, Marisa makes her choice. She accepts the accounting job, and six months later she is posted to New York.

## The Desirability Curve: A Scoring Shortcut

Marisa had only four consequences to consider, so assigning the initial desirability scores was fairly easy. When you have many possible consequences, however, the assignment of desirability scores can become difficult and time consuming. Fortunately, there is a shortcut: the desirability curve. After plotting the desirability scores of a few representative consequences—five, typically—you connect them on a graph to form a curve. You can then use this curve to determine the desirability scores of all other possible consequences.

There's one important limitation to the use of desirability curves: you can use them only when each of the consequences can be expressed using a single, numerical variable, such as dollars, acres, years, or lives saved. They can be used, for example, to chart the payoffs of investments in terms of dollars made or lost, the potential environmental impact of a proposed development in terms of square miles affected, or the possible consequences of open-heart surgery in terms of years added to the patient's life.

Desirability curves can be so useful, however, that it will often be worthwhile to use the even swap method to convert consequences described by multiple variables into a single, numerical term. (Remember that Karen, the accident victim, did this in the Application at the end of Chapter 7. She converted the time and psychological impacts of a trial into equivalent dollar amounts, enabling her to describe her consequences using a single variable: money.)

**An Investment Example.**    To see how desirability curves work, consider the decision problem facing Jim Nance. Jim makes his family's investments, guided by the dual objectives of growth and preservation of capital. Through an investment club, he now has the opportunity to make a one-year investment of $10,000 in a private venture, unrelated to the securities markets, on which he can make as much as 87.5 percent or lose as much as 37.5 percent. In other words, over the year, his $10,000 could grow to $18,750 or shrink to $6,250. Before learning of this opportunity, Jim had planned to buy an insured one-year certificate of deposit (CD) paying 6 percent interest, which would deliver a sure $10,600 in a year.

While the potential payoffs of $18,750 and $6,250 represent the extremes for the private-venture investment, Jim knows that there are a multitude of other possible payoffs between the extremes, and that each will have its own probability of occurring. Using a simple software program and drawing on publicly available industry data, Jim and some of his fellow investment clubbers develop a risk profile for the investment, showing a range of possible payoffs (which can be used to describe both the outcomes and consequences in this case) and their chances. The risk profile is represented by the first two columns of the table on page 144. Analyzing the risk profile, Jim sees that each of the first three payoffs in the list would all lose money, making the overall

## Risk Profile for Jim Nance's
## Potential Investment

| Chance | Outcome and Consequence: Monetary Payoff | Contribution to Average Monetary Payoff |
|---|---|---|
| 2% | $ 6,250 | $    125.00 |
| 6 | 7,500 | 450.00 |
| 13 | 8,750 | 1,137.50 |
| 15 | 10,000 | 1,500.00 |
| 18 | 11,250 | 2,025.00 |
| 17 | 12,500 | 2,125.00 |
| 11 | 13,750 | 1,512.50 |
| 9 | 15,000 | 1,350.00 |
| 4 | 16,250 | 650.00 |
| 3 | 17,500 | 525.00 |
| 2 | 18,750 | 375.00 |
| 100% | Average monetary payoff: | $11,775.00 |

chance of suffering a loss 21 percent (2 + 6 + 13). On the other hand, the last seven payoffs earn more than the CD, making the chance of beating the CD's return 64 percent (18 + 17 + 11 + 9 + 4 + 3 + 2).

The risk profile for this decision is clear and unambiguous (numbers usually are), but the decision isn't. Should Jim invest in the risky venture, or should he go for the safe CD?

To answer that question, most financial analysts would first compute the "average monetary payoff" of the private-venture investment. To do this, they'd simply multiply the dollar amount of each payoff by its chances, as shown in the last column of the table, and then they'd add up all the resulting figures to arrive at the average payoff. In Jim's case, the average monetary payoff of the venture investment is $11,775. Because this amount is only $1,125 higher than the $10,600 that would be delivered by the CD, many financial analysts would advise Jim to take the CD. They would reason that a sure 6 percent return is too good to turn down given the high risk of the private venture.

There's a big problem with this approach, however. It doesn't take into account the risk tolerance of Jim and his family. It may be that the potential gain of the private venture is worth the risk to Jim. This may be so even if, like most people, he is risk averse and the loss of a given amount of money may have a far greater impact on his family than the gain of that same amount.

The desirability curve can deal with this. What you do is:

- Construct a desirability curve (often referred to in the literature as a utility curve) that assigns a desirability score to each payoff that reflects the subjective desirability of money to you.
- Use the desirability scores of the possible payoffs and their chances to calculate an overall desirability score for each alternative.
- Choose by comparing the overall desirability scores of the alternatives.

We'll show you how this is done for Jim Nance's investment.

**Create a Desirability Curve.**    Because Jim is working with numbers, ranking the consequences is easy. When it comes to money, more is better, so he just assigns 100 to the highest payoff, $18,750, and 0 to the lowest, $6,250. Now, to avoid having to figure out the desirability scores for such a large number of consequences, Jim plots a desirability curve.

He uses a simple graph, illustrated below, with the horizontal axis showing the range of possible payoffs (the consequences) and the vertical axis showing the desirability score associated with each payoff. He first plots the two extreme points: point *A* represents the score of 0, assigned to $6,250, and point *B* represents 100, assigned to $18,750. These mark, respectively, the beginning and the end of the curve. He then uses his judgment to establish a midpoint for the curve corresponding to a desirability score of 50. Since preservation of capital is a prime objective, Jim decides that going from $6,250 to $9,000 is as desirable as going from

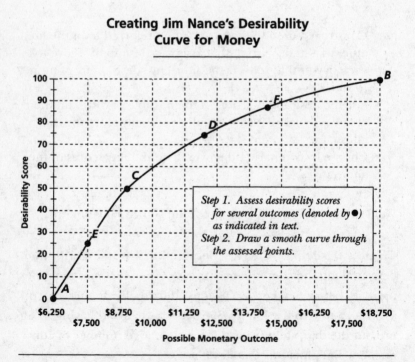

**Creating Jim Nance's Desirability Curve for Money**

Step 1. Assess desirability scores for several outcomes (denoted by ●) as indicated in text.

Step 2. Draw a smooth curve through the assessed points.

$9,000 to $18,750. He thus assigns a desirability score of 50 to $9,000 (point $C$).

Jim uses similar thinking to divide the ranges above and below $9,000 into equally desirable ranges to establish payoffs for the 25 and 75 scores. He assigns 75 to $12,000 (point $D$), which he decides is the midway desirability point between $9,000 and $18,750. He assigns 25 to $7,500 (point $E$), his midway desirability point between $6,250 and $10,000.

Usually, connecting just five points will produce a smooth, easy-to-read curve. If more points are needed, however, the ranges can be divided into new equally desirable ranges. To better define his curve, Jim adds a sixth point by establishing the desirability midpoint, point $F$, between points $D$ and $B$, at $14,500. Its desirability score is 87.5, halfway between 75 and 100. He then connects the six points, producing the desirability curve (page 146).

The curve represents the desirability scores of all the potential payoffs falling between $6,250 and $18,750. Reading from the curve, the desirability score assigned to the certificate of deposit alternative, which has a monetary value of $10,600, is 65, for example. Before using the curve, though, Jim decides it would be wise to test some of its implications and, if necessary, adjust it. The curve implies that, for Jim, the following increases, representing desirability increments of 25, are equivalent: $6,250 to $7,500; $7,500 to $9,000; $9,000 to $12,000; and $12,000 to $18,750. Asking himself whether these increments reflect his true feelings about desirability and risk, Jim concludes that they do.

**Use the Desirability Curve to Make a Decision.**    Jim is now ready to evaluate the proposed investment, taking into account his risk tolerance. First, he reads from the curve the desirability scores that correspond to the 11 payoffs, and he writes the scores on his risk profile, as shown in the table below. He then multiplies each payoff's chances by its desirability score, as in the last column. Finally, he adds up the resulting figures to calculate an overall desirability score for the investment.

The resulting overall desirability score is 68.35. Since this exceeds the desirability of 65 from the certificate of deposit, Jim should choose the private-venture investment.

**Get Additional Insights by Converting Desirability Scores Back to Money.**   Converting the overall desirability score back into

### Computing the Overall Desirability Score for Jim Nance's Potential Investment

| Consequence: Payoff in a Year | Chance | Desirability Score | Contribution to Average Desirability |
|---|---|---|---|
| $ 6,250 | .02 | 0 | 0 |
| 7,500 | .06 | 25 | 1.50 |
| 8,750 | .13 | 46 | 5.98 |
| 10,000 | .15 | 60 | 9.00 |
| 11,250 | .18 | 70 | 12.60 |
| 12,500 | .17 | 78 | 13.26 |
| 13,750 | .11 | 84 | 9.24 |
| 15,000 | .09 | 90 | 8.10 |
| 16,250 | .04 | 94 | 3.76 |
| 17,500 | .03 | 97 | 2.91 |
| 18,750 | .02 | 100 | 2.00 |
| | 1.00 | Overall desirability score: | 68.35 |

money yields new insights and another way to think about making risky decisions involving a single objective. Take Jim's risk profile for the venture as an example.

- Its 68.35 desirability score corresponds to a monetary value of $11,000 from Jim's desirability curve. This says that the value of the venture to Jim is $11,000.
- Having a monetary value gives Jim an intuitive feeling for how much better the private venture is. Namely, it is worth $400 more to him than the certificate of deposit, worth $10,600.
- The values assigned to risk profiles can be used for decision making. A more risk averse member of Jim's investment club might value the private venture at $10,000 and, as a result, choose the certificate of deposit.
- Someone who had no risk aversion at all would value the private venture as its average monetary payoff, $11,775 (see table on page 144). Jim's value is less because he is risk averse. The difference between the average monetary payoff and Jim's value, $775, is called his *risk adjustment* for the risk profile.
- For a given risk profile, the risk adjustment is an indicator of your risk aversion. The larger the risk adjustment for any given risk profile, the more risk averse you are and vice versa.

It may be tempting to assign a value directly to a risk profile without introducing desirabilities in a formal way. Using your intuition, you could directly assess a risk adjustment, then subtract it from the average monetary value to obtain the value of the risk profile to you. This might seem simple and direct, but you need incredibly good intuition to do it well. To arrive at an appropriate figure, somehow you would have to keep in mind all the payoffs and how desirable you consider each of them to be, as well as how likely each is. This is mind boggling.

The desirability curve approach breaks this thought process into manageable bites, allowing you first to carefully think about your desirabilities, then to blend them with probabilities to calculate an appropriate value.

**Interpret Desirability Curves.**  Jim's curve not only helps him make a specific decision, it also provides him with considerable insight into his attitude toward financial decision making in general. It shows, for instance, that avoiding the largest possible loss (that is, the loss from $10,000 to $6,250), with its desirability score of 60, outweighs obtaining the maximum gain (going from $10,000 to $18,750), which represents a 40-point score. Avoiding losses, it is clear, weighs more heavily in Jim's decision making than achieving equivalent gains, indicating that he is risk averse.

In fact, the shape of your desirability curve is a very good indicator of your overall risk tolerance, as the figure on page 151 illustrates. An upwardly bowed curve indicates a risk-averse attitude with a greater risk aversion indicated by a greater curvature. A straight line represents a risk-neutral attitude, and a downwardly bowed curve connotes a risk-seeking attitude.

## Watch Out for These Pitfalls

We've shown you some reliable, logical ways to account for your risk tolerance in making decisions. By using them, you can avoid being tripped up by old habits and other common pitfalls. Here are a few to watch out for:

## Interpreting Risk Attitude from a Desirability Curve

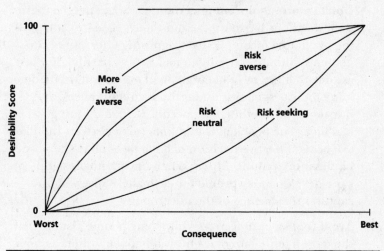

- **Don't overfocus on the negative.** To avoid bad consequences (and the resulting regrets), some people give disproportionate attention to the downsides of their alternatives. They focus on avoiding trouble, even if it's unlikely to occur. In many cases, however, the upside potential will far outweigh the downside risk. *Lesson:* Consider the full range of consequences, not just the bad ones.

- **Don't fudge the probabilities to account for risk.** Some people, consciously or unconsciously, account for their risk tolerance by raising the probabilities of outcomes with bad consequences and lowering the probabilities with good ones—just to be safe. Every risk profile is thereby shaded toward a pessimistic view, and the resulting decision is likely to be overly cautious. *Lesson:* Judge chances on their own merits, without regard for your risk tolerance. Account for your risk tolerance separately.

- **Don't ignore significant uncertainty.**  Some people make their decisions based on the most likely scenario, attempting to eliminate complexity by ignoring uncertainty altogether. Without bothering to make a risk profile, they just assume that the most likely chain of events will occur, determine their best choice under those circumstances, and pursue it. If something else occurs, well, that's just good or bad luck. The problem is that something else *can* and likely *will* occur. Effective decision making takes all viable possibilities into account. *Lesson:* When uncertainty is significant, develop a risk profile for each alternative which captures the essence of the uncertainty.

- **Avoid foolish optimism.**  While some people assume that the most likely chain of events will happen, others assume that a very positive chain of events will happen. They see decisions through rose-colored glasses. Their wishful thinking may be a personality trait—we all have friends and associates who are perennially optimistic—but often it is simply due to a lack of thoroughness in thinking about what could occur. They might project the completion date for a project, for example, without thinking through all the possible delays. *Lesson:* Think hard and realistically about what can go wrong as well as what can go right.

- **Don't avoid making risky decisions because they are complex.**  Overwhelmed by complexity, some people throw up their hands. They may do nothing and live with the status quo, they may make a random or arbitrary decision, or they may get someone else to decide for them. Such "decisions," unfortunately, will rarely be consistent with their objectives. *Lesson:* Don't despair; you *can* deal sensibly with complexity and reach a smart choice.

- **Make sure your subordinates reflect your organization's risk tolerance in their decisions.**    Government agencies, businesses, civic groups, families, and other organizations all have institutional risk tolerances. Without guidance and the proper incentives, people in an organization may, by their decisions, either expose the organization to too much risk or forfeit attractive opportunities by acting too conservatively. *Lesson:* An organization's leaders should take three simple steps to guide subordinates in dealing successfully with risk. First, sketch desirability curves that reflect the risk-taking attitude of the organization. Second, communicate the appropriate risk tolerance by issuing guidelines that include examples of how typical risky decisions should be handled. Third, examine the organization's incentives to ensure they are consistent with the desired risk-taking behavior.

## Open Up New Opportunities by Managing Risk

In making decisions at home and at work—especially financial ones—you may frequently find yourself facing a risk that exceeds your comfort level. If so, there may be ways to manage this risk to make it acceptable to you. Consider the situation of Harry Healy, a small business owner who makes a good living in the very risky business of drilling and producing shallow natural gas wells near Zanesville, Ohio. Harry faces enormous risks each time he drills a well. If it produces no gas, he can lose all of the $125,000 cost of drilling. Furthermore, the price of natural gas can fluctuate by as much as 300 percent in a single year.

Fortunately, Harry has learned to apply various techniques, used regularly by people dealing in the financial markets, to manage his risks. Like Harry, you should consider adding these techniques to your risk management repertoire.

**Share the risk.**    When a good opportunity feels too risky, share the risk with others.

In Harry's case, the risk profile for drilling a typical well shows a substantial downside risk, including a 10 percent chance of finding no gas, a 30 percent chance of recovering only a small percentage of the drilling costs, and a 20 percent chance of losing a modest amount. He breaks even about 10 percent of the time and thus actually makes money only about 30 percent of the time—though the profits in these cases can be substantial.

With a net worth of under $750,000, Harry is unwilling to risk $125,000 at a time, when the chances are 40 percent that he will lose all or most of his investment. He manages the risk, therefore, by sharing it with a group of investors, each of whom takes a proportional share of the costs and any earnings. Harry himself invests $25,000, a sum he is comfortable with, to keep 20 percent of each well.

**Seek risk-reducing information.**    Try to temper risk by seeking information that can reduce uncertainty.

To reduce his risk, Harry targets drilling sites with better-than-average risk profiles. He routinely studies surface geology, information on gas production at nearby wells, and, for borderline sites, he orders a seismic test, costing about $12,000, which can reduce some of the uncertainty about whether and how much natural gas might be present.

**Diversify the risk.**    Avoid placing all your eggs in just a few baskets. Look for ways to diversify.

Harry diversifies his assets, investing some in stocks and bonds, rather than subjecting them all to the vagaries of the gas business. In addition, by buying mutual funds rather than individual securities, he lowers his risk further, because mutual funds hold a number of securities, and the ups of some cancel the downs of others. Even on vacation, Harry diversifies. When he goes white-water rafting through wilderness areas, his party divides the food among each raft.

**Hedge the risk.** When fluctuations in market prices or rates (interest rates, exchange rates, and the like) expose you to discomforting risk, look for ways to hedge.

Fluctuations in the price of natural gas can result in large swings in Harry's monthly income, and a few successive months of low prices can have serious repercussions. By buying contracts on the commodities exchange that put a floor on future prices, he can—at a cost—manage this risk. Alternatively, he can sign annual fixed-price contracts with the utilities that buy his gas. Harry typically sells over half of his gas at fixed prices and risks leaving the rest subject to market fluctuations.

**Insure against risk.** Whenever a risk consists of a significant but rare downside, with no upside, try to insure against it. But don't overinsure.

Harry would be liable for substantial damage and injuries from a well blowout or other accident. Although the chances of such an occurrence are extremely low, a serious accident could wipe him out. Harry manages this risk by insuring against it. He doesn't, on the other hand, insure his $18,000 pickup truck against collision or theft. Because he can afford such a loss, he figures the insurance isn't worth its cost.

All of these techniques help to manage risk by enlisting others in transactions that reshape the original risk profile, making it more compatible with the decision maker's risk tolerance. So, when you face an uncomfortable risk, ask yourself, "What transactions can I make with others that will improve my risk profiles?"

APPLICATION

### To Settle or Not to Settle?

Karen and her advisor, Jane, have come down to the final element of Karen's decision: her need for money, which determines her attitude toward risk. Starting with the assumption that Karen, otherwise broke and in debt, has at a minimum assets equal to $210,000 (the settlement offer minus her lawyer's fees), Jane begins to examine how Karen would use the money. How would it change her life? Karen is ready with answers.

"I've thought about that a lot. First I'd pay off my debts: a $50,000 student loan, $25,000 for the surgery my health insurance didn't cover, and $8,000 in taxes. Then I'd have some purely cosmetic surgery to make these facial scars less visible, and with any money left over, I'd get a used car and maybe pay more rent somewhere to get out of my dreadful apartment."

"How's your job? How much do you make?"

"It's a dead-end job, you know that. I hate sales, and I only earn about $25,000 a year. I'd like to go back to school and learn something that would help me get a better job. I'd have to take time off, anyway, for the surgery."

Jane summarizes. "If you go to trial and lose—not the most likely outcome, but it has a chance of 30 percent—your life would be pretty bad. You'd be in debt; you couldn't afford some of the things that would make you happier; you'd have to remain in your present job and keep your present apartment."

Karen interrupts. "Not to mention the humiliation of losing and my regret over not accepting the sure thing of $210,000. I'm in pretty bad shape now, but I'd be far worse off if I lost the trial."

"But who says you're going to lose the trial?" Sam barks.

Jane continues: "If you netted a lot more money from the trial, what would you do with it? How would it change your life? How much happier would you be?"

"If I had a lot more money, I'd still do all the things I said I'd do if I had the $210,000. But I'd get a condo rather than go on renting, I'd buy a new car instead of a used one, and maybe I'd buy some clothes and take a few trips to Europe and other places. And I'd definitely go to graduate school. But those things aren't nearly as important to me as what that initial $210,000 would bring."

"How much more money above the first $210,000 would give you roughly the same satisfaction it would?"

"Close to a million! At least $800,000."

Sam couldn't contain himself. "You can't be serious, Karen! You can't equate having only about $200,000 with having another $800,000!"

"Yes, I am serious. Without the $210,000, I'm ruined. More would make me richer, but that's not as important to me as getting an even start.

"This has really helped me," Karen says, turning to Jane. "When you force me to think about my attitude toward risk and the probabilities involved, not only do I see clearly that I should accept the $210,000 offer, but I have firm conviction in that decision. When I think about how I'd use the money, the peace of mind I'd get, I know that the possibility of gaining more in court isn't worth the gamble of losing it all."

On the courthouse steps, before Sam could accept the $300,000 offer, the other side increased it to $325,000. Despite his strongly differing opinion on what she should do, Sam accepted on Karen's behalf.

## Lessons from the Application

Karen couldn't identify the smart choice until she had examined her risk tolerance. But once she had thought hard about the relative desirability to her of various possible consequences, she was able to make a deci-sion without further analysis. This is the case for most of the uncertainty decisions that most of us face. Using a little careful, qualitative thinking about the significance of the consequences almost always makes the smart choice obvious.

If Karen had been unable to decide after thinking through the risks and benefits qualitatively, she could use the desirability scoring method. She would assign scores to the possible consequences, compute the overall desirability of going to court and of settling, and base her deci-sion on what the scores revealed.

Sam's sharp disagreement with Karen about whether to accept the $300,000 offer reflected a correspondingly sharp difference in risk toler-ance. (They agree on probabilities; after all, Sam was the source of these judgments.) With Karen's risk tolerance, settling was the smart choice, but with Sam's, settling was foolishly conservative.

It is good to have our advisors challenge our thinking on risk toler-ance (as Sam did), but in the final analysis, it's our own (or, in this case, Karen's) risk attitude that matters in making a decision. You should cer-tainly seek out information and guidance from informed advisors, but you should never let them make a decision for you. Sam's recommenda-tion to go to court was incompatible with Karen's risk tolerance.

# CHAPTER 9

# Linked Decisions

Many important decision problems require you to select now among alternatives that will greatly influence your decisions in the future. Your choice of a college major, for example, may strongly influence your future career options. Such decisions are *linked decisions*—to make the smartest choice about what to do now, you need to think about what you might decide to do in the future.

All decisions affect the future, of course. Karen's decision, at the end of the last chapter, to take the settlement offer in her lawsuit will obviously affect her future options and opportunities. But those will be essentially new decision situations. The kinds of decisions we want to talk about here involve a *necessary* connection between the current decision and one or more later ones. A doctor initiating treatment on a critically ill patient, for example, has to think about how to respond to possible complications and how the current treatment may open or foreclose alternative treatments in the future.

In such linked decisions, the alternative selected today creates the alternatives available tomorrow and affects the relative desirability of those future alternatives. Linked decisions can be years apart, as with the choice of a college major and the subsequent choice of a career. Or they can be minutes apart, as with a series of choices about which route to take when driving to work during rush hour. In all cases, though, they add a new layer of complexity to decision making.

## Linked Decisions Are Complex

Here's a business example. Imagine that you're the marketing director for a juice company, and you're in charge of the launch of a promising new fresh-fruit drink made with added vitamins. You know that the success of the drink will hinge on its marketing concept—the combination of name, price, packaging, advertising, and so forth that will define the product in the marketplace. By creating an image of the drink in consumers' minds, the concept will have tremendous influence over who buys the drink and in what quantity.

Your original concept for the beverage was as a thirst quencher for young adults. Market research indicated that the concept was a viable one—it had a good chance of succeeding with the targeted consumers. But the research also revealed signs that a different concept, not yet fully developed, could be even more successful. This concept would require a slight reformulation of the product and a market approach targeting it as an energy drink for active adults 25 to 55 years of age.

Which concept—thirst quencher or energy drink—should you choose? Each presents uncertainties concerning sales. As an energy drink, the product could far outsell the thirst quencher, but if it flopped, the failure would likely be greater as well.

In evaluating the desirability of each concept, you need to think about possible future decisions. If, for example, the product's initial sales are disappointing, how might you turn them around? A different advertising campaign? More money for price promotions at retail outlets? If the thirst quencher has low sales, you might be able to reformulate it as an energy drink and market it to the older age group. A failed energy drink, however, would be unlikely to appeal to young adults as a thirst quencher, no matter how it was reformulated or repackaged. Your choice of concept is thus linked to these future decisions.

Before actually choosing a concept, you could, of course, decide to conduct market research on the energy drink. The research would reduce the uncertainty about potential sales, providing more information for making a smarter choice on the concept. But it would cost a lot of money and delay introduction of the new drink, giving competitors more time to come up with competing products. Would it be worth it?

The situation you face contains all the elements of linked decisions:

- A *basic decision* must be addressed now (which concept).
- The desirability of each alternative in the basic decision is influenced by uncertainties (how well each would sell).
- Relative desirability is also influenced by a future decision (how to possibly turn an unsuccessful product introduction into a successful product) that would be made after the uncertainty in the basic decision is resolved (data received on initial sales of the drink).
- An opportunity exists to obtain information (market re-

search on the energy drink concept) before making the basic decision. This information could reduce the uncertainty in the basic decision and, one would hope, improve the future decisions—but at a cost (in money and time).

- The typical decision-making pattern is a string of decide, then learn; decide, then learn more; decide, then learn; and so on.

## Relationships among Linked Decisions

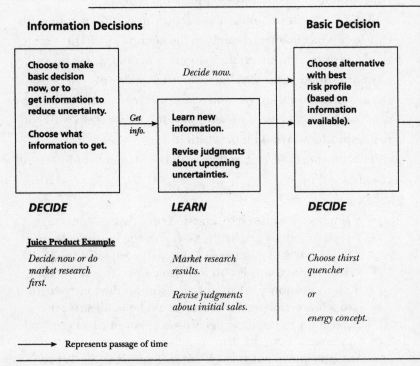

**Information Decisions**

**Basic Decision**

Choose to make basic decision now, or to get information to reduce uncertainty.

Choose what information to get.

*Decide now.*

*Get info.*

Learn new information.

Revise judgments about upcoming uncertainties.

Choose alternative with best risk profile (based on information available).

***DECIDE***      ***LEARN***      ***DECIDE***

<u>Juice Product Example</u>

*Decide now or do market research first.*

*Market research results.*

*Revise judgments about initial sales.*

*Choose thirst quencher*

*or*

*energy concept.*

⟶   Represents passage of time

# Make Smart Linked Decisions by Planning Ahead

Making smart choices about linked decisions requires under-standing the relationships among them. The decisions linked to a basic decision can take two forms:

- *Information decisions* are pursued before making the basic decision. They are linked because the information you obtain helps you make a smarter choice in the basic decision.

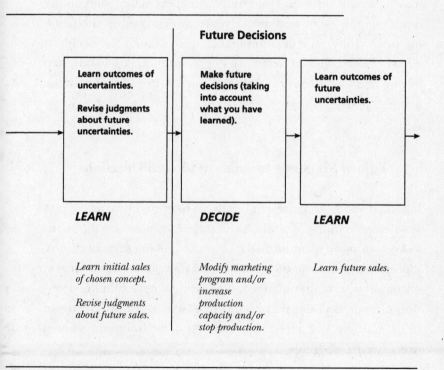

- *Future decisions* are made after the consequences of a basic decision become known. They are linked because the alternatives that will be available in the future depend on the choice made now.

By plotting out these relationships as a decide-learn sequence (see figure on page 163), you are able to clarify the sequence of decisions and see how each one will influence the others.

*The essence of making smart linked decisions is planning ahead.* Makers of effective linked decisions, like successful chess players, plan a few decisions ahead before making their current decision. After making a basic decision (your move as a chess player) and noting developments (your opponent's move, which resolves the pending uncertainty), the decision maker again plans a few decisions ahead before making the next choice. Continuing to do this, step by step, moves the series of decisions toward the fulfillment of the decision maker's objectives.

## Follow Six Steps to Analyze Linked Decisions

Linked decisions can present hundreds or even thousands of possible combinations of alternatives and outcomes—far too many to keep in mind all at once. The trick to making such decisions, therefore, is to size up the situation and then focus your attention on those aspects that matter most. By creating a simplified version of your decision that retains its essential features, you can think sensibly and effectively about it. The following six-step process will help guide you.

**Step 1: Understand the basic decision problem.** Begin with the first three core elements of our general approach: define the *problem,* specify *objectives,* and generate *alternatives.* Then identify the uncertainties that influence the *consequences* of the alternatives. The uncertainties are the crux of linked decisions. Without them, there would be no reason to link decisions in decide-learn sequences, because there would be nothing to learn between decisions.

Draw up a list of the uncertainties. Then narrow the list down, selecting the few uncertainties, maybe just one or two, that most influence consequences. These uncertainties are candidates for developing risk profiles, if necessary, in future steps. For less significant uncertainties, make a reasonable assumption of how they will turn out. There is no need to do a full analysis of every uncertainty confronting you. For instance, in the marketing example, how well the juice will sell is the dominant uncertainty. In comparison, uncertainties about production costs are minor, so a reasonable assumption about costs will do.

**Step 2: Identify ways to reduce critical uncertainties.** Getting information before deciding means becoming proactive about the learning portion of the decide-learn sequence. You consciously defer making a basic decision in order to seek information that can reduce or resolve future uncertainties and thus improve your basic decision. A politician, for instance, believing his chances of winning a city council election to be excellent, tentatively plans to run. But if new information reveals his support to be weaker than he believed, he may need to reconsider his decision.

To create information-gathering strategies, you need to decide *what* information is important and *how* to gather it:

- For each critical uncertainty, list the kinds of information that could reduce your uncertainty, and then determine how your view of the decision might change in the face of the new information. The politician, for example, could reduce his uncertainty about his support if he had clear data about his name recognition and his standing among voters. If fewer than half of the voters recognized his name and, of those, fewer than half viewed him favorably, he might conclude that his chances of winning were poor and reverse his tentative decision to run.
- Think about ways to obtain the important information. To collect information on voter attitudes, the politician could conduct a telephone poll or a series of focus groups.

Having decided what information to consider getting and how to get it, the next issue concerning information is *whether* it is worth getting it before making your basic decision. That comes in step 5.

**Step 3: Identify future decisions linked to the basic decision.**     To identify relevant future decisions, you need to ask what decisions would naturally follow from each alternative in your basic decision. If the politician decides not to run, for example, he will need to consider his next moves. Should he throw his support behind another candidate? Should he work to bolster his name recognition by seeking an appointed office? Should he start working and raising money toward the next election? For your linked decisions, list all the future decisions you can think of, then winnow the list to the few that seem most significant.

How far ahead should you look when considering potential future decisions? Not too far. Look for a natural time horizon—

where future decisions are only weakly linked to the consequences of your basic decision. In most cases, include your basic decision and, at most, two future decisions. Keep it simple.

**Step 4: Understand relationships in linked decisions.**   You can draw a decision tree to represent the links between choices and learned information in sequence. The tree should include the basic decision and any important information decisions and future decisions linked to it. Here are a few suggestions for drawing a decision tree:

- **Get the timing right.**   What happens when? What comes before what? When will key information become available? When can decisions be made? Organize your answers into a table, a timeline, or a figure like that on page 163 to help you understand the flow of information, events, and decisions. Anticipating the timing of and the order in which decisions should be made and information gathered is fundamental to making effective linked decisions.

- **Sketch the essence of the decision problem.**   Use your notes to construct a decision tree. Start on the left with information choices (if any) and outcomes, then fill in the middle by defining your basic decision, and finally complete the right side of the tree with future decisions and uncertainties associated with them. Keep the tree simple so it's easier to understand. Later you can add further details, such as additional possible outcomes of uncertainties or additional alternatives, as the case requires.

- **Describe the consequences at the end points.**   The end points on the tree represent the consequences of having followed a particular sequence of alternatives and outcomes. Use the ideas in Chapters 5 and 7 to describe

the consequences of each sequence in terms of your fundamental objectives, keeping in mind what can happen in the
future and what has already happened along the way.

**Step 5: Decide what to do in the basic decision.**    To "solve" your
basic decision problem, you want to think ahead and then work
backward in time. The decision tree will help you. Start at the end
of the tree (the right side) and work backward. At each decision
point, think hard and decide what choice you would make when
and if you ever reach that point. Lop off the branches representing the alternatives not taken. Continue working backward until
you reach the individual alternatives for the basic decision. You
will now have made a plan for each alternative so you will be able
to evaluate it more clearly.

If, in the course of planning, you find it tough to decide what
to do at some future decision point, you may need to quantify
your tradeoffs, uncertainties, or risk tolerance using the techniques described in Chapters 6 through 8. But remember: quantify only as necessary. Quantify one element at a time and check
after each to see if a decision has become obvious.

Deciding what to do in your basic decision includes deciding
what information, if any, to collect before making the basic decision. To do this, first recall the lists you composed in step 2. Then,
for each item on the lists, estimate the costs and benefits of gathering the information. Costs typically include money, effort, time,
discomfort, and delay. To understand what benefit you might derive from additional information, you must know what you would
choose if you didn't gather the information; new information is
of benefit only if it might change a decision. If you'd make the

same basic decision regardless of the information learned, then the information isn't worth gathering. A good quick test to weed out information-gathering alternatives is to ask what you'd pay to completely resolve the uncertainty. If an information alternative costs more, it's an obvious noncontender.

**Step 6: Treat later decisions as new decision problems.** The clock moves ahead. Having chosen an alternative for your basic decision (the thirst quencher) and having learned something (it's not selling well), what should you do? However well you've prepared earlier, when you actually reach subsequent decision points, you should rethink the situation. Your circumstances and perspective may have changed, and, due to the passage of time, you can now see further ahead from this point than you could before. Take advantage of new knowledge to enhance your understanding of your new decision problem and improve your plan. What was once a future decision is now a new basic decision.

## Keep Your Options Open with Flexible Plans

Sometimes uncertainty is so great and the present environment so changeable that it is difficult to plan future decisions with confidence. Emergency room doctors, firefighters, newsroom editors, and business managers are among those who often find themselves in such fast-developing situations. In these cases, you should consider developing *flexible plans* that allow you to make the most of whatever circumstances arise. Flexible plans keep your options open. They can take a number of forms:

- **All-weather plans.** Like all-weather tires, all-weather plans work well in most situations, but they are seldom the optimal choice for any one situation. They represent a compromise strategy. In highly volatile situations, where the risk of outright failure is great, an all-purpose plan is often the safest plan.

- **Short-cycle plans.** With this strategy, you make the best possible choice at the outset, then reassess that choice often. Business managers do this when they develop a one-year plan but update it quarterly, taking into account business developments in the interim.

- **Option wideners.** Sometimes the best plan is to act in a way that expands your set of future alternatives. If a computer manufacturer had only one chip supplier, for example, it might consider widening its supplier list, purchasing, say, 90 percent of its chips from its regular source and 5 percent from each of two new sources. Then, if the established supply line were interrupted, alternatives could be developed sooner. It might cost the manufacturer a little more to buy from three vendors, but in the long run it could save the company's business.

- **"Be prepared" plans.** These backup plans stress preparedness—having a reasonable response available for most contingencies. Many people, for example, keep a first aid kit and basic medications in the medicine cabinet for emergencies and a bottle of wine or a pitcher of iced tea in the refrigerator in case friends drop by. As the old expression has it, "Success is what happens when preparation meets opportunity."

## Should Dan Change Jobs?

Dan Morgan must make up his mind quickly. His current job is deteriorating, but an intriguing new job offer presents complications.

Dan, age 52, and his wife Doris, age 45, have two children: Sarah, 16, a high school sophomore, and Nick, 13, an eighth-grader, both in public school. They live in a comfortable house in the Boston suburb of Arlington. Doris, an elementary school teacher, works in a nearby town. She feels burnt out by the disciplinary demands of her job and, at an annual salary of $42,000, underpaid.

Dan, a computer specialist—not an engineer or computer scientist, and that's a problem—sells software for Omega Software. Once a high-flier, Omega is now mired in hard times. It has laid off a number of salespeople over the last three years, and Dan thinks it's only a matter of time before they get around to firing him or trying to entice him into early retirement.

Dan makes an annual salary of $50,000 plus commissions and bonuses, which have run as high as $40,000 in past years but have tumbled lately to $15,000. Still, with Doris's salary, the Morgans feel financially comfortable. But what if Dan lost his job? A comparable one would not be easy to find at his age.

Enter a new possibility. Dan has often worked with Bill Brown, part owner of an up-and-coming computer networking company, DotCom Communications, in Amherst, Massachusetts—about 100 miles away. Brown has offered Dan a job in software and systems sales at an annual salary of $60,000, plus commissions that would range from $10,000 to $40,000 per year. DotCom is growing, and Dan feels that, should he take the job, his future would be relatively secure. DotCom needs to hire someone fast, so Dan has only a week—at most, three—to decide whether to take the job.

Dan and Doris work together to make all serious decisions affecting the family—and this one certainly qualifies as serious. They sit down and get to work.

## Objectives

Dan and Doris compile a list of objectives, considering everything they can think of that contributes to the happiness of the family:

- Quality of work for Dan
- Quality of work for Doris
- Dan's pay
- Doris's pay
- Dan's job security
- Quality of housing for the family
- Culture and amenities, mostly for Dan and Doris
- Quality of education for Sarah
- Quality of education for Nick
- Social life and recreational activities for Sarah
- Social life and recreational activities for Nick

## Alternatives

The Morgans recognize that they have two basic alternatives: to *Stay,* in which Dan refuses the DotCom offer and hopes to keep his current Omega job, or to *Change,* in which Dan accepts DotCom's offer and the family hopes to make it turn out well for all of them.

The family is torn. Sarah and Nick strongly advocate staying in Arlington, even though they realize that if their dad loses his job it will affect them severely. They may be forced to work part-time to help support the family; summer vacation plans will be drastically altered; and, most importantly, their choice of college may be seriously limited. Doris has mixed feelings. Even though she would like to leave her job, Arlington has been her home for many years, and both Dan's and her elderly parents live nearby. Dan tilts toward the move. For him, it represents the excitement of new challenges and a fresh start after a long period of job worries.

## Uncertainties

Dan and Doris are both overwhelmed by the uncertainties they must confront.

- How secure is Dan's present job? Will his commissions grow, hold steady, or continue to diminish? Will he be laid off or forced into retirement? If so, when?
- If Dan takes the new job, how much traveling will he have to do? Will he be up to it? How reliable are the commission estimates? Dan likes Brown, but he'll also have to work with Brown's partner, Jack Carney, who seems moody and unfriendly. Will they get along?
- If the family moves, will Doris find a satisfying job in the Amherst area?
- Sarah, upset at the prospect of the move, doesn't want to leave Arlington. How will she adjust? Will the Amherst school system be comparable to her current one? Sarah takes cello lessons, and she's made outstanding progress. Will she be able to continue with quality instruction?
- How will Nick adjust? He excels in the honors science and computer programs at his middle school, and he has his heart set on playing football for Arlington High. How will the science and sports programs in Amherst compare with what he has enjoyed in Arlington?

## Information Decisions

To help resolve the impasse, Doris comes up with a creative alternative: *Explore.* To pursue this alternative, Dan investigates the possibility of taking an unpaid leave from Omega to work for DotCom on a short-term trial basis. He would gain some information—but also take on additional uncertainties. Omega would give Dan a six-month unpaid leave, after which they would probably—but not certainly—rehire him *if* a pending contract renewal with one of its key clients, the Department of Defense (DOD), comes through in August. If Dan stays with Omega and Omega gets the DOD contract, Omega will guarantee Dan's further employment for at least three years. DotCom would, in turn, reluctantly accept a temporary arrangement, but it will not guarantee the job to Dan after the six-month trial. He would have the inside track, but Dot-Com would reserve the right to consider other candidates.

The Morgan family must decide in the next week if it wants to adopt the Explore strategy: a six-month leave without guarantees. The family has given some thought to how it would live for the next several months if Dan took the DotCom job either outright or temporarily. Because it is now February, the middle of the school year, they would remain in Arlington until June. Dan's commute would be two hours each way, so he would get a studio apartment near DotCom. One or two days a week, Dan could stay home in Arlington and telecommute by fax and modem; he would have to be away from home only three or four days per week.

Doris would take an upcoming school holiday to investigate jobs in Amherst and surrounding communities. Also, if the Explore alternative is selected, the family would sublet a house in the area for the summer. This would give everyone time to get some idea of what a move might entail. If, after the summer, Sarah were to remain adamant about staying in Arlington, she could live during the school year with a good friend of hers until she graduated from high school. Meanwhile, during the summer, her parents would try to woo her to their new home with horseback riding lessons. If the family were to move next September, Nick would have to go with them: he would not be given the choice that Sarah has. Amherst's football program may not be as good as Arlington's, but he would likely get to play even if the family moved.

## Timeline

If the family decides on either Change or Explore, by August it will know something about Dan's new job, Doris's job possibilities, and the children's responses. They will also know if the DOD has renewed Omega's contract.

At the end of August, with this additional knowledge, Dan will have another round of choices—future decisions. If he has stayed with Omega and the DOD contract has not come through, he'll lose his job; he could then try to see if DotCom still had a job available. If he has moved to DotCom and the family or he thinks it has been a mistake, and if the DOD contract has been renewed, he could approach Omega to rehire him. If he has chosen Explore, depending on the circumstances, he might decide either to return to Omega or to stay with DotCom.

By the beginning of September, Dan should have learned whether he has a job and where. If, in September, he ends up with neither job, he will try to get another job somewhere else. At his salary level and with the competition from younger talent, however, the pickings will be slim.

Dan and Doris summarize the sequence of decisions and learning that must take place over the ensuing nine months in the timeline shown on pages 176–177.

### Decision Tree

To further help them in their decision, Dan draws a decision tree—shown on page 178—that shows the sequencing of decisions to be made and the information learned along the way from now through early September. He indicates each decision with a square box, each uncertainty with a circle, and each consequence with a letter.

Dan and Doris take a hard look at the decision tree. Their first decision (decision 1) has three alternatives: Stay with Omega, Change to DotCom, or Explore (a temporary move to DotCom using a six-month leave from Omega.) If Dan were to Stay, he would learn in mid-August whether Omega's DOD contract had been renewed (uncertainty 4). If yes, he would continue to work for Omega (decision 8). If no, he would lose his job at Omega, and he would then see if the job with DotCom were still available (decision 9), finding out the answer in early Septem-

## A Timeline for the
## Morgan Family Decision

| February | February–June | July–August | August |
|---|---|---|---|
| *Decide* | *Learn* | *Learn* | *Learn* |
| **Stay with Omega** | | | DOD contract? |
| **Explore** | Quality of job at DotCom: travel? Carney? | | |
| | Teaching job opportunities? Substitute teacher jobs? | | |
| | | Quality of living? Housing, amenities? | |
| | | Sarah's adjustment? | |
| | | Nick's adjustment? | DOD contract? |
| **Change to DotCom** | Quality of job at DotCom: travel? Carney? | | |
| | Teaching job opportunities? Substitute teacher jobs? | | |
| | | Quality of living? Housing, amenities? | |
| | | Sarah's adjustment? | |
| | | Nick's adjustment? | DOD contract? |

ber (uncertainty 16). If yes, he takes the job. The consequence of following this path is labeled *B*. If no job is available, the consequence would be *C*—presumably at this point he would be in deep trouble, and he would have to look for another job, which he might not find.

If Dan chose the Change alternative at decision 1, he would know by the beginning of August whether working at DotCom and living in Amherst suits his family (uncertainty 3). If the situation is bad, and the DOD project comes through for Omega (uncertainty 7), Dan would approach Omega for his old job (decision 14). If the contract doesn't come through, Dan, with consequence *Q*, will continue at DotCom but begin looking for a new job.

Even the more complex set of circumstances of the Explore alternative can be clearly followed using the decision tree.

| Early September | September | After September |
|---|---|---|
| *Decide* | *Learn* | *Decide and Learn* |
| If "no" DOD, try DotCom | DotCom's reaction | If "no" on Omega and DotCom, try for new job |
| If "yes" on DOD, DotCom or Omega | DotCom and Omega reactions | If "no" on Omega and DotCom, try for new job |
| If "yes" on DOD, DotCom or Omega | DotCom and Omega reactions | If "no" on Omega and DotCom, try for new job |

After tracing each branch of the tree, Dan and Doris take a break for a well-earned cup of coffee. "Well, darling," Dan says, "what should we do?"

"The tree's been very helpful," Doris responds. "It shows our decision problem at a glance—what we know and don't know, when more information will become available, and what we do next. But it leaves out my career and the kids' adjustment."

"Those things are very important, of course, but to keep the tree workable, I combined them under the grand uncertainty: What's good or bad for the family as a whole?"

"So where are my and the kids' concerns taken into account in this decision tree?" Doris asks.

"Your concerns, as well as mine, and the impacts of our decision on

## A Decision Tree for the Morgan Family Decisions

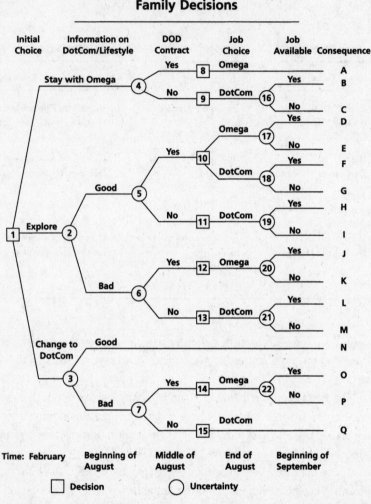

| Initial Choice | Information on DotCom/Lifestyle | DOD Contract | Job Choice | Job Available | Consequence |
|---|---|---|---|---|---|

Time: February | Beginning of August | Middle of August | End of August | Beginning of September

☐ Decision     ◯ Uncertainty

the family as a whole are accounted for by consequences *A* through *Q* at the end of the decision tree," Dan explains. "Each of these consequences should summarize how well off we are having traveled along the corresponding path of alternatives and outcomes in the tree."

"I see. Consequence *A* for the family is great, *B* is OK, and *M* is awful. But some are a lot more uncertain than others. Take *E*. We explore, get good vibes from DotCom, the DOD contract materializes, and you approach Omega, but they've given the job to someone else. So with *E* you would try to get DotCom to make a long-term commitment. But what if they won't?"

"That's the penalty they're imposing to get me to accept their offer now."

"And it may work out that you're happy with them but they aren't so happy with you," Doris teases.

Dan smiles. "I suppose so. OK, life goes on with *E*. We could always extend the tree out from there, grow it taller—except that it's on its side—or bushier, with more options. What we really need to do is to rate *A* through *Q* on how desirable they are to us, as a family. I think that would be easy to do."

"If we stay, we have to be scared stiff of ending up with *C*."

"And if we move, we could end up with disastrous consequences *P* or *Q*. But these still aren't as bad as *C*, since I can keep my job at DotCom even if we all hate it. What we need to think about, it seems, are two things: first, how likely are the uncertainties? And, second, what is the relative desirability of the various consequences?"

"Agreed," says Doris.

"If we can't decide just using this tree to think things through, we're going to have to quantify some things to really see how they compare. But we shouldn't have to quantify everything—just enough to decide. As I see it, we have two key uncertainties in our situation. I've thought pretty hard about them, trying to assign probabilities. Ready?"

Doris nods, and Dan continues. "First, what's the chance that Omega will get the DOD contract? I'd been thinking it was an even-money bet, but most people around the office think that's optimistic. So I dropped my estimate to about 30 percent."

"That's disturbing. I'd been thinking that the chances were closer to 80 or 90 percent. For me, that makes our choice much clearer."

"Yes," Dan agrees, "I thought it would. And the probability for my second key uncertainty might be the clincher."

"That's where you explore, like what you find, and end up asking DotCom to make the arrangement permanent?"

"Exactly. I have to say that the chances are around 25 percent that they would refuse. They might find someone else better or cheaper, or decide that I'm not as good as they think. I might not get along with Carney, and he might blackball me. Yeah, 25 percent sounds right."

"That's enough for me," Doris says. "I know what I want to do. I'm going to write down my choice."

"I guess I know, too: We opt to accept DotCom outright. Is that what you wrote down?"

"It sure is. But I have some process advice. Let's tell the kids and our folks our decision, but hold off telling Omega and DotCom for a few days. Let's see how we sleep the next few nights. If we have second thoughts, then, as much as I hate to do it, maybe we'll need to do a bit more quantification."

### Lessons from the Application

Dan and Doris approached their linked decision problem in a manner consistent with the six-step process outlined in this chapter. Let's review their experience to see the process in action.

- **Step 1: Understand the basic decision problem.** The Morgans' basic decision was whether Dan should stay at Omega or change jobs to work for DotCom. Talking things through, Dan and Doris listed objectives for each family member, as well as the dozen or so uncertainties they faced. They then reduced the uncertainties to just four, to focus their problem and make it more manageable.

- **Step 2: Identify ways to reduce critical uncertainties.** Dan and Doris developed the Explore alternative as a means of gathering information about several of the uncertainties they faced. By taking a temporary position with DotCom and by spending the summer in Amherst, the family would get information relevant to them all. A lot of creative thought and negotiation went into fashioning the Explore alternative to be acceptable to Omega and DotCom.

  The Morgans focused on only one Explore alternative, although others could have been developed. Dan might have tried working for DotCom without moving to Amherst for the summer, or the family might have moved for the summer while Dan maintained his job at Omega. Dan could also have sought another job in the Boston area while remaining at Omega, but he chose to keep it simple and not to add that alternative to the problem.

- **Step 3: Identify future decisions linked to the basic decision.** After the basic decision about a job now, the Morgans included future decisions about the possible need to switch jobs again based on whether the initial choice was working out or still available. Since this information would become clear by the end of the summer, they chose September as their time horizon.

- **Step 4: Understand relationships in linked decisions.** To get the timing in the problem straight, the Morgans constructed a timeline, which helped Dan sketch a decision tree. Following the Explore branch, Dan could have drawn a dozen or so learning outcomes, depicting what each member of the family might learn. To keep the decision tree simple, however, he chose to include only two branches: a good or bad outcome for the family.

  In the Morgans' tree, only one branch was exhibited at each of the decision points from 8 to 15—except for point 10, where the choice between Omega and DotCom was not obvious. Not including alternatives that are obviously poor choices avoids unnecessarily complicating the tree.

  The Morgans felt they could easily visualize the consequences at each end position and therefore didn't need to write out the consequences in detail. Instead, they talked about how good or bad some of the consequences would be. They were scared stiff about ending up with consequence C on the decision tree, for example, because of the bleak job-hunting prospects in the future.

- **Step 5: Decide what to do in the basic decision.**     By thinking ahead and working back, the Morgans clarified their choices in their basic decision. For the alternative "Stay with Omega," the plan would be to stay if Omega got the DOD contract and to approach DotCom for a job if it didn't. If that didn't work out, Dan would try to find work elsewhere.

  The Morgans faced many uncertainties, but Dan and Doris were able to make their basic decision after quantifying just two: the chance of the DOD contract award and the chance that DotCom would hire Dan if he chose the Explore alternative. Their judgments about these probabilities gave them the confidence to go forward without further quantification. But, occasionally, your decisions may require more quantification, perhaps to the extent of using the even swap method (see Chapter 6) to make tradeoffs between consequences.

- **Step 6: Treat later decisions as new decision problems.**     Dan and Doris opted in February for the DotCom job and the move to Amherst. By late August, however, they've learned a lot. Dan isn't completely happy with his new job: there's too much traveling, and Carney is a pain in the you-know-what. Doris is ecstatic, though: she's found a job as a substitute teacher in Holyoke, near Amherst, and in her spare time plans to take courses in history at the University of Massachusetts, working toward an advanced degree that will allow her to teach high school. Sarah has broken up with her boyfriend in Arlington and would just as soon move far, far away. Nick, preparing to enter high school, has attended football tryouts but doesn't much like the coach, and he misses the kids on his old block. The family hasn't yet put its Arlington house on the market. Omega, to everyone's surprise, was awarded the DOD contract. Dan thinks he can get his old job back. Should he try?

  Our advice to him is to consider this as a new decision. Dan and Doris should rethink the family's situation, looking further into the future and examining in more detail those aspects that matter now.

## Maintain Your Perspective

Building an awareness of linked decisions is a good news–bad news situation. The bad news is that, because they are so complex, linked decisions will be among the most difficult you will face—and, typically, they will also be among the most important. The good news is that, as complexity and importance increase, the value of systematic, qualitative thinking also increases significantly. Just knowing how sets of decisions are linked and using a modest amount of foresight can help considerably in making a smart choice and can practically guarantee avoiding many, if not all, of the dumb ones.

So, maintain your perspective. Your comfort level with your choices may not be as high on linked decisions as on simpler ones, but your accomplishments may be much greater. Skiing the beginner slopes is relatively easy, but skiing the expert runs gives you a much greater sense of accomplishment—even if your form is less than perfect. Over time, making *smart* choices on linked decisions will affect your life and career more positively and profoundly than making *perfect* choices on all your simpler decisions put together.

# CHAPTER 10

# Psychological Traps

THIS WHOLE BOOK HAS BEEN ABOUT how to think systematically about tough, important decisions. By now you're much better prepared to identify and avoid the eight most common and most serious errors in decision making:

- Working on the wrong problem
- Failing to identify your key objectives
- Failing to develop a range of good, creative alternatives
- Overlooking crucial consequences of your alternatives
- Giving inadequate thought to tradeoffs
- Disregarding uncertainty
- Failing to account for your risk tolerance
- Failing to plan ahead when decisions are linked over time

But, in addition to these process mistakes, there's an entirely different category of errors that can undermine even the most carefully considered decisions. We call these errors "psychological traps." They arise because our minds sometimes play serious tricks on us.

For half a century psychologists and decision researchers have been studying the way our minds function when we make decisions. This research, in the laboratory and in the real world, has revealed that we develop unconscious routines to cope with the complexity inherent in most decisions. These routines, known as *heuristics,* serve us well in most situations. In judging distance, for example, our minds often rely on a heuristic that relates clarity with closeness. The clearer an object appears, the closer it must be. The fuzzier it appears, the further away it must be. This simple mental shortcut helps us to make the continuous stream of distance judgments required to navigate the world.

Yet, like most heuristics, it isn't foolproof. On days that are hazier than normal, our eyes will tend to trick our mind into thinking that things are more distant than they actually are. Because the resulting distortion poses few dangers for most of us, we can safely ignore it. For airline pilots, though, the distortion could be catastrophic. That's why pilots always use objective measures of distance in addition to their vision.

Researchers have identified a whole series of such flaws in the way we think. Some, like the clarity heuristic, take the form of sensory misperceptions. Others take the form of biases. Others appear simply as irrational anomalies in our thinking. What makes all these traps so dangerous is their invisibility. Because most are hard-wired into our thinking process, we fail to recognize them— even when we're falling right into them.

Though we can't rid our minds of these ingrained flaws, we can learn to understand the traps and compensate for them. In this chapter, we examine some of the most common psychological traps and how they affect decision making. By familiarizing yourself with them and the diverse forms they take, you'll be better able to ensure that the decisions you make are sound and reliable. *The best protection against these traps is awareness.*

## Overrelying on First Thoughts: The Anchoring Trap

How would you answer these two questions?

- Is the population of Turkey greater than 35 million?
- What's your best estimate of Turkey's population?

If you're like most people, the figure of 35 million cited in the first question—a figure that we chose arbitrarily—influenced your answer to the second question. Over the years, we've posed these questions to many groups of people. In half the cases we use 35 million in the first question; in the other half we use 100 million. Without fail, the answers to the second question increase by many millions when the larger figure is used in the first question. This simple test illustrates the common and often pernicious mental phenomenon known as *anchoring*. In considering a decision, the mind gives disproportionate weight to the first information it receives. Initial impressions, ideas, estimates, or data "anchor" subsequent thoughts.

Anchors take many guises. They can be as simple and seemingly innocuous as a comment offered by your spouse or a statistic appearing in the morning newspaper. They can be embedded in the wording of your decision problem. One of the most common types of anchors is a past event or trend. A forecaster attempting to project the number of patients who will visit a medical clinic next January often begins by looking at the number who visited last January. The historical number becomes the anchor, which the forecaster then adjusts based on other factors. Although this approach may often lead to a reasonably accurate estimate, it tends to give too much weight to the past figure and not enough weight to other factors. Particularly in situations characterized by rapid change, the historical anchor can lead to poor forecasts and, in turn, to misguided choices.

Whatever their source, anchors often prejudice our thinking in ways that prevent us from making good decisions. Because anchors have the effect of establishing the terms on which a decision will be made, they are often used by savvy negotiators as a bargaining tactic. Say you've been looking for a work of art to hang over the fireplace in your living room. You visit a local art dealer and see on display a unique and compelling painting by an unknown young artist—a work that has no clear market value (and no price tag!). You estimate its worth at approximately $1,200, but when you begin talking about the painting with the dealer, he immediately suggests a price of $2,800. As an opening gambit, that price may be designed to anchor you, to shift your sense of the piece's worth upward. If you respond by attempting to bargain down from $2,800, the final cost may be unduly influenced by the dealer's initial proposal—the anchor.

**What can you do about it?**   The effect of anchors in decision making has been documented in thousands of experiments. Anchors influence the decisions of everyone—doctors, lawyers, managers, homeowners, students. No one can avoid their influence; they're just too widespread. You can, however, reduce their impact by using the following techniques:

- Always view a decision problem from different perspectives. Try using alternative starting points and approaches rather than seizing on and sticking with the first line of thought that occurs to you. After exploring various paths, reconcile any differences in their implications.
- Think about the decision problem on your own before consulting others, to avoid becoming anchored by their ideas.
- Seek information and opinions from a variety of people to widen your frame of reference and push your mind in fresh directions. Be open-minded.
- Be careful to avoid anchoring other people from whom you solicit information and counsel. Tell them as little as possible about your own ideas, estimates, and tentative decisions. If you say too much, you may simply get back your own preconceptions (which have become your advisors' anchors).
- Prepare well before negotiating. You'll be less susceptible to anchoring tactics.

## Keeping on Keeping On: The Status Quo Trap

You inherit 100 shares of a blue-chip stock that you would never have bought yourself. You can sell the shares and reinvest the money for a minimal commission and no tax consequences. What will you do?

When faced with this situation, a surprising number of people hang on to the inherited shares. They find the status quo comfortable, and they avoid taking action that would upset it. "Maybe I'll rethink it later," they say. But later is always later.

In fact, most decision makers display a strong bias toward alternatives that perpetuate the current situation. On a broad scale, we can see this tendency at work whenever a radically new product is introduced. The first automobiles, revealingly called "horseless carriages," looked very much like the buggies they replaced. The first "electronic newspapers" appearing on the World Wide Web looked very much like their print precursors.

Many psychological experiments have shown the magnetic attraction of the status quo. In one, a group of people were randomly given one of two gifts—half received a decorated mug, the other half, a large Swiss chocolate bar. They were then told they could effortlessly exchange the gift they received for the other gift. You might expect that about half would have wanted to make the exchange, but only one in ten actually did. The status quo exerted its power even though it had been arbitrarily established only minutes before!

Other experiments have shown that the pull of the status quo is even stronger when there are several alternatives to it as opposed to just one. More people choose the status quo when there are two alternatives to it, *A* and *B*, than when there is only one, *A*. Why? Choosing between *A* and *B* requires more effort.

**What can you do about it?**   First of all, remember that, in any given decision, maintaining the status quo may indeed be the best choice—but you don't want to choose it just because it *is* the status quo. Use these techniques to lessen the pull of the present:

- Always remind yourself of your objectives and examine how they would be served by the status quo. You may find that elements of the current situation are incompatible with those objectives.

- Never think of the status quo as your only alternative. Identify other options and use them as counterbalances, carefully evaluating all their pluses and minuses.
- Ask yourself whether you would choose the status quo alternative if, in fact, it weren't the status quo.
- Avoid exaggerating the effort or cost involved in switching from the status quo.
- Put the status quo to a rigorous test. Don't simply compare how the status quo *is* with how the other alternatives *would be*. Things can change with the status quo, too.
- If several alternatives are clearly superior to the status quo, don't default to the status quo because you have a hard time picking the best one. Force yourself to choose one.

## Protecting Earlier Choices:
## The Sunk-Cost Trap

Three months ago, your eight-year-old car suddenly required serious engine repairs. Faced with spending $3,000 on the engine work or junking the car and buying a new one, you chose the repairs. Now, however, your transmission's shot, and fixing it will cost you another $1,500. Alternatively, you could sell the car as is for $1,000 and buy a new one. You know that the car will likely require further expensive repairs in the future, though you hope it won't happen soon. What will you do?

If you're like most people, you'll decide to fix the transmission, not wanting to "lose" the $3,000 you already spent on the engine. But that's the wrong reason for the choice! Would you make the same choice if the engine repair had (miraculously) been done for free? Almost certainly not—yet that's how you should think about the problem. What matters now is the current condition of the car and the economic pros and cons of the two alternatives. The past is past; what you spent then is irrelevant to your decision today.

As this example illustrates, we tend to make choices in a way that justifies past choices, even when the past choices no longer seem valid. Our past decisions create what economists term "sunk costs"—old investments of time or money that are now unrecoverable. We know, rationally, that sunk costs are irrelevant to the present decision, but nevertheless they prey on our psyche, leading us to make wrong-headed decisions. We may have refused, for example, to sell a stock or a mutual fund at a loss, forgoing other, more attractive investments. Or we may have poured enormous effort into improving the performance of an employee whom we know we shouldn't have hired in the first place. Remember, your decisions influence only the future, not the past.

Why can't people free themselves from past decisions? Sometimes it's just fuzzy thinking. But frequently it's because they are unwilling, consciously or not, to admit to a mistake (even if the "mistake" was caused by bad luck rather than a bad decision). Acknowledging a decision that's gone awry may be purely a private matter, involving only one's self-esteem, but in many cases it's a very public matter, inviting critical comments or negative assessments from friends, family members, colleagues, or bosses. If you fire your poorly performing recent hire, you're making a public admission of poor judgment. It seems psychologically safer to let him stay on, even though all you're doing is compounding the error.

**What can you do about it?**    For all decisions with a history, you will need to make a conscious effort to set aside any sunk costs—

whether psychological or economic—that will muddy your thinking about the choice at hand. Try these techniques:

- Seek out and listen carefully to the views and arguments of people who weren't involved with the earlier decisions and hence are unlikely to have a commitment to them.
- Examine why admitting to an earlier mistake distresses you. If the problem lies in your own wounded self-esteem, deal with it head on. Remind yourself that even smart choices can have bad consequences and that even the most experienced decision makers are not immune to errors in judgment. Remember the wise words of the noted investor Warren Buffet: "When you find yourself in a hole, the best thing you can do is stop digging."
- If you worry about being second-guessed by others, make this consequence an explicit part of your decision process. Also consider how you would explain your new choice to these people.
- If you fear sunk-cost biases in your subordinates at work, pick one who was previously uninvolved to make the new decision. (See the example below.)

---

**Avoiding the Sunk-Cost Bias:**
**Reassigning Bankers**

The sunk-cost bias shows up with disturbing regularity in banking, where it can have particularly dire consequences. When a borrower's business runs into trouble, a lender will often advance additional funds in hopes of providing the business with some breathing room to recover. If the business does have a good chance of coming back, that's a good investment. Otherwise, it's throwing good money after bad.

Fifteen years ago, we helped a major U.S. bank recover after making many bad loans to foreign businesses. We found that bankers responsible for originating the problem loans were far more likely to advance additional funds—repeatedly, in many cases—than were bankers who took over the accounts after the original loans were made. Too often, the original bankers' strategy—and loans—ended in failure. Having been trapped by an escalation of commitment, they had tried, consciously or unconsciously, to protect their earlier, flawed decisions. They had fallen victim to the sunk-cost trap. The bank finally solved the problem by instituting a policy requiring that a loan be immediately reassigned to another banker as soon as any problem became serious. The new banker would be able to take a fresh, unbiased look at whether offering more funds had merit.

## Seeing What You Want to See: The Confirming-Evidence Trap

For a while you've been concerned that the stock market has gone too high, and you've all but decided to sell most of your portfolio and invest the cash in a money market mutual fund. But before you call your broker, you decide to do one more thing to check the wisdom of selling. You call a friend, who you know sold out her portfolio last week, to find out her reasoning. She presents a strong case for an imminent market decline. What do you do?

You'd better not let that conversation be the clincher, because you've probably just fallen into the confirming-evidence trap. This trap leads us to seek out information that supports our existing instinct or point of view while avoiding information that contradicts it. What, after all, did you expect your friend to give other than a strong argument in favor of her own decision?

The confirming-evidence trap not only affects where we go to collect evidence, but also how we interpret the evidence we do receive, leading us to give too much weight to supporting information and too little to conflicting information. If you had read an article on the stock market in an investing magazine, for example, you would have tended to be less critical of arguments in favor of selling stock and more critical of arguments in favor of remaining in the market.

In one psychological study of this phenomenon, groups opposed to and supporting capital punishment read two reports of careful research on the effectiveness of the death penalty. One report concluded that the death penalty was effective; the other concluded that it was not. In spite of being exposed to solid scientific information supporting counterarguments, the members of both groups became *even more convinced* of the validity of their own position after reading both reports. They automatically accepted the supporting information and dismissed the conflicting information.

There are two fundamental psychological forces at work here. First is our tendency to subconsciously decide what we want to do before we figure out why we want to do it. Second is our tendency to be more engaged by things we like than by things we dislike—a tendency well documented even in babies. Naturally, then, we are drawn to information that confirms our subconscious leanings.

**What can you do about it?**    It's not that you shouldn't make the choice toward which you're subconsciously drawn. It's just that you want to be sure it's the smart choice. You need to put it to the test. Here's how:

- Get someone you respect to play devil's advocate, to argue against the decision you're contemplating. Better yet, build the counterarguments yourself. What's the strongest reason to do something else? the second strongest reason? the third? Consider the position with an open mind.
- Be honest with yourself about your motives. Are you really gathering information to help you make a smart choice, or are you just looking for evidence confirming what you think you'd like to do?
- Expose yourself to conflicting information. Always make sure that you examine all the evidence with equal rigor and understand its implications. And don't be soft on the disconfirming evidence.
- In seeking the advice of others, don't ask leading questions that invite confirming evidence.

### Posing the Wrong Question: The Framing Trap

A young priest asked his bishop, "May I smoke while praying?" The answer was an emphatic "No!" Later, encountering an older priest puffing on a cigarette while praying, the younger priest scolded, "You shouldn't be smoking while praying! I asked the bishop, and he said I couldn't."

"That's strange," the older priest replied. "I asked the bishop if I could pray while I'm smoking, and he told me that it was okay to pray at any time."

As this old joke shows, the way you ask a question can profoundly influence the answer you get. The same is true in decision making. If you frame your problem poorly, you're unlikely to make a smart choice.

In a recent case involving automobile insurance, framing made a $200 million difference. To reduce insurance costs, two neighboring states, New Jersey and Pennsylvania, made similar changes in their laws. Each state gave drivers a new option: by accepting a limited right to sue, they could lower their premiums. In New Jersey you automatically got the limited right to sue unless you specified otherwise, but in Pennsylvania the choice was framed so that you automatically got the full right to sue unless you specified otherwise. In New Jersey, about 80 percent of drivers chose the limited right to sue, while in Pennsylvania only 25 percent chose it. The different frames in this case established different status quos, creating biases that in large part determined consumers' behavior. As a result, Pennsylvania failed to gain approximately $200 million in expected insurance and litigation savings.

Clearly, much depends on how you ask the question. Psychologists have even shown that when *the same question* is framed two different ways—ways that are objectively equivalent—people choose differently. Why? Because each framing makes different objectives more salient.

Decision researchers have documented two types of frames that distort decision making with particular frequency.

**Framing as gains versus losses.**   In one experiment, patterned after a classic study by decision researchers Daniel Kahneman and Amos Tversky, we explored the impact of framing by posing the following problem to a group of experienced insurance professionals:

You are a marine property adjuster charged with minimizing the loss of cargo on three insured barges that
sank yesterday off Alaska. Each barge holds $200,000
worth of cargo, which will be lost if not salvaged within
72 hours. The owner of a local marine salvage company gives you two options, both of which will cost the
same:

> Plan A: This plan will save the cargo of one of the
> three barges, worth $200,000.
>
> Plan B: This plan has a one-third probability of sav-
> ing the cargo on all the barges, worth $600,000, but
> has a two-thirds probability of saving nothing.

Which plan would you choose?

If you're like 71 percent of the respondents in the study, you
chose the "less risky" plan *A,* which will save one barge for sure.
Another group in the study, however, chose between alternatives
*C* and *D:*

> Plan C: This plan will result in the loss of two of the
> three cargoes, worth $400,000.
>
> Plan D: This plan has a two-thirds probability of result-
> ing in the loss of all three cargoes and the entire
> $600,000, but has a one-third probability of losing no
> cargo.

Faced with this choice, 80 percent of respondents preferred plan *D.*

The pairs of alternatives are, of course, equivalent—plan *A* is
the same as plan *C,* and plan *B* is the same as plan *D*—they've just
been framed in different ways. The strikingly different responses

reveal that people are risk-averse when a problem is posed in terms of gains (barges saved) but risk-seeking when a problem is posed in terms of avoiding losses (barges lost). Furthermore, they tend to adopt the frame as it is presented to them rather than re-stating the problem their own way.

**Framing with different reference points.**    The same problem can also elicit very different responses when frames use different reference points. Let's say you have $2,000 in your checking ac-count, and you are asked the following question:

> Would you accept a 50-50 chance that offered the pos-sibility of either losing $300 or winning $500?

What if you were asked *this* question:

> Would you prefer keeping your current checking ac-count balance of $2,000 to accepting a 50-50 chance that would result in your having either $1,700 or $2,500 in your account?

Once again, the two questions pose the same problem. Although your answers to both questions should, rationally speaking, be the same, studies have shown that many people would refuse the 50-50 chance in the first question but accept it in the second. Their different reactions result from the different reference points of the two frames. The first frame, with its reference point of 0, emphasizes incremental gains and losses, and the thought of losing triggers a conservative response in many people's minds. The second frame, with its reference point of $2,000, puts things into perspective by emphasizing the broader financial impact of the decision.

**What can you do about it?**    A poorly framed problem can undermine even the best-considered decision. But the effect of improper framing can be limited by imposing discipline on the decision-making process:

- Remind yourself of your fundamental objectives, and make sure that the way you frame your problem advances them.
- Don't automatically accept the initial frame, whether it was formulated by you or by someone else. Always try to reframe the problem in different ways. Look for distortions caused by the frames.
- Try posing problems in a neutral, redundant way that combines gains and losses or embraces different reference points. For example:

    Would you accept a 50-50 chance that offered the possibility of losing $300, resulting in a bank balance of $1,700, or winning $500, resulting in a bank balance of $2,500?

- Think hard throughout your decision-making process about the framing of the problem. At points throughout the process, particularly near the end, ask yourself how your thinking might change if the framing changed.
- When your subordinates at work recommend decisions, examine the way they framed the problem. Challenge them with different frames.

## Being Too Sure of Yourself:
## The Overconfidence Trap

What's your forecast for the average temperature in your city tomorrow? How sure are you about your estimate? Now predict a high value, one for which you think there's only a 1 percent chance that the actual average temperature will exceed, and a low value, one for which you think there's only a 1 percent chance that the actual average will fall below. In other words, set a range such that there is a 98 percent chance that the actual average temperature will fall between your low and high figures.

If you make many, many estimates of this sort and your self-appraisal of your estimating skills is good, statistically you should expect that only about 2 percent of the time would the actual value fall outside your assessed ranges. Unfortunately, that's *not* what hundreds of experiments have shown. Typically, the actual value falls outside the range 20 to 30 percent of the time, not 2 percent! Overly confident about the accuracy of their prediction, people set too narrow a range of possibilities.

Think of the implications. If you underestimate the high end or overestimate the low end of a range of values for a crucial variable (such as potential sales) and you act accordingly, you may expose yourself to far greater risk than you realize—or you may miss out on wonderful opportunities.

A major cause of overconfidence is anchoring. When you make an initial estimate about a variable, you naturally focus on mid-range possibilities. This thinking then anchors your subsequent thinking about the variable, leading you to estimate an overly narrow range of possible values.

**What can you do about it?**   To reduce the effects of overconfidence:

- Avoid being anchored by an initial estimate. Consider the extremes (low and high) first when making a forecast or judging probabilities.
- Actively challenge your own extreme figures. Try hard to imagine circumstances in which the actual figure would fall below your low or above your high, and adjust accordingly. For example, if your forecast is 80 degrees and your high figure is 88, how might the high turn out to be 95?
- Challenge any expert's or advisor's estimates in a similar fashion. They're as susceptible as anyone to this trap. Suppose you're the president of a company considering the launch of a new product, and your marketing manager says that there's only a 1 percent chance that you will sell less than 35,000 units of the product next year. You might ask, "What if it sells only 20,000, what could have happened?" His response: "A competitor might have come out with an improved version of its product." You then ask, "What's the chance of that occurring?" He says, "Oh, about 10 percent." If there is a 10 percent chance of selling around 20,000 units, there is certainly more than a 1 percent chance of selling less than 35,000. Your marketing manager anchored on business as usual, meaning no new competitive products, in making his original estimates.
- Do your homework. Substitute facts for opinion whenever possible. They're immune to overconfidence!

## Focusing on Dramatic Events:
## The Recallability Trap

What's the probability of a randomly selected jet flight on a major U.S. airline ending in a fatal crash?

What's your answer? If you're like most people, you will have overestimated the probability. The actual chance of such a crash? According to statistics provided by researchers at MIT, it is only about one in 10,000,000!

Because human beings infer the chances of events from experience, from what we can remember, we can be overly influenced by dramatic events—those that leave a strong impression on our memory. We all, for example, exaggerate the probability of rare but catastrophic occurrences, such as plane crashes, because they get disproportionate attention in the media. A dramatic or traumatic event in your own life can also distort your thinking. You will assign a higher probability to traffic accidents if you've passed one on the way to work, and you will assign a higher chance to someone's dying of cancer if a close family member or friend has died of the disease.

In fact, anything that distorts your ability to recall events in a balanced way will distort your probability assessments or estimates. In one experiment, lists of well-known men and women were read to different groups of people. Each list had an equal number of men and women, but on some lists the men were more famous than the women while on others the women were the more famous. Afterward, the participants were asked about the percentage of men and women on each list. Those who had heard the list with the more famous men thought there were more men on the list, while those who had heard the list with the more famous women thought there were more women.

**What can you do about it?**     To minimize this type of error,

- Each time you make a forecast or estimate, examine your assumptions so that you are not being unduly swayed by memorability distortions.
- Where possible, try to get statistics. Don't rely on your memory if you don't have to.
- When you don't have direct statistics, take apart the event you're trying to assess and build up an assessment piece by piece. For example, to estimate the likelihood that a scheduled airline flight will result in a fatality, put together a statistic for the average number of fatal airline crashes per year in the United States with a rough estimate (derived from an Internet reservations system, perhaps) of the number of flights per year in the United States. The resulting probability may not be as accurate as that of the MIT study, but it's better than relying on your unaided memory.

## Neglecting Relevant Information: The Base-Rate Trap

Donald Jones is either a librarian or a salesman. His personality can best be described as retiring. What are the odds that he is a librarian?

When we use this little problem in seminars, the typical response goes something like this: "Oh, it's pretty clear that he's a librarian. It's *much* more likely that a librarian will be retiring;

salesmen usually have outgoing personalities. The odds that he's a librarian must be at least 90 percent." Sounds good, but it's totally wrong.

The trouble with this logic is that it neglects to consider that there are far more salesmen than male librarians. In fact, in the United States, salesmen outnumber male librarians 100 to 1. Before you even considered the fact that Donald Jones is "retiring," therefore, you should have assigned only a 1 percent chance that Jones is a librarian. That is the *base rate*.

Now, consider the characteristic "retiring." Suppose half of all male librarians are retiring, whereas only 5 percent of salesmen are. That works out to 10 retiring salesmen for every retiring librarian—making the odds that Jones is a librarian closer to 10 percent than to 90 percent. *Ignoring the base rate can lead you wildly astray.*

**What can you do about it?**    Analyze your thinking about decision problems carefully to identify any hidden or unacknowledged assumptions you may have made. Use these suggestions as guides:

- Don't ignore relevant data; make a point of considering base rates explicitly in your assessment.
- Don't mix up one type of probability statement with another. (Don't mix up the probability that a librarian will be retiring with the probability that a retiring person is a librarian.)

## Slanting Probabilities and Estimates:
## The Prudence Trap

You are a researcher on a team designing a medical program to respond to a potential cancer-causing agent. Having reviewed the empirical data and relevant literature, you think that the probability that the potential carcinogen actually leads to cancer is on the order of 1 in 100, but you don't know for sure. What probability should you give?

Many people in this situation might think it *prudent* to slant the probability from 1 in 100 to, say, 1 in 20, just to be "safe." But if several such judgments are to be made and if they are all similarly slanted and then cascaded together, all in the spirit of prudence, the result may be a hopelessly distorted understanding of the seriousness of the problem. The recommended response will most likely be far more costly or drastic than is warranted.

As this example shows, even one of our best decision-making impulses—caution—can lead us into error. Consider the methodology of "worst-case analysis," which was once popular in the design of weapons systems and is still used in certain engineering and regulatory settings. Using this approach, weapons were designed to operate under the worst possible circumstances, even though the odds of those circumstances actually coming to pass were infinitesimal. Worst-case analysis added huge costs with no practical benefit, proving that too much prudence can lead to inappropriate decisions.

In business, the cascading nature of the prudence trap can be disastrous. A number of years ago, for example, one of the Big Three U.S. automakers was deciding how many of a new-model car to produce in anticipation of its busiest sales season. The market planning department, responsible for the decision, asked other departments to supply forecasts of key variables such as anticipated sales, dealer inventories, competitor actions, and costs. Knowing the purpose of the estimates, each department slanted its forecast to favor building more cars—"just to be safe." But the market planners took the numbers at face value and then made their own "just-to-be-safe" adjustments. Not surprisingly, the number of cars produced far exceeded demand, and the company took six months to sell off the surplus, resorting in the end to deep price cuts.

**What can you do about it?**    For sound decision making, honesty is the best policy.

- State your probabilities and give your estimates *honestly*. In communicating to others, state that your figures are not adjusted for prudence, or for any other reason.
- Document the information and reasoning used in arriving at your estimates, so others can understand them better.
- Emphasize to anyone supplying you with information the need for honest input.
- Vary each of the estimates over a range to assess its impact on the final decision. Think twice about the more sensitive estimates.

## Seeing Patterns Where None Exist: The Outguessing Randomness Trap

At the gaming table, the dice seem to be running hot. The last four rolls produced four sevens in a row. Is this the time to bet heavily on seven? Or, perhaps, after four straight sevens, does it make sense to bet heavily against seven?

Your lucky cousin selects a number for you to bet in your state lottery. Does this increase your chances of winning?

The answer to these questions—and many like them—is a resounding "No!"

Despite our innate desire to see patterns, random phenomena remain just that—random. Dice and lotteries have neither memory nor conscience—every roll, every number choice is a new and different event, uninfluenced by all previous events. If a run of sevens affected the next throw of the dice in a predictable way, casinos would go broke.

**What can you do about it?**   To avoid distortions in your thinking, you must curb your natural tendency to see patterns in random events. Be disciplined in your assessments of probability.

- Don't try to outguess purely random phenomena. It can't be done.
- If you think you see patterns, check out your theory in a setting where the consequences aren't too significant. If you think you have a system to beat the gaming tables or the stock market by capitalizing on past results, try it out with fake money. Use your system on a long record of past data, wagering your hypothetical stake. (A computer buff familiar with simulation techniques would be a big help.) The exercise will save you lots of real money!

## Going Mystical about Coincidences:
## The Surprised-by-Surprises Trap

John Riley is a legend. On two separate occasions he has won a
one-in-a-million lottery. The chance of that happening is so rare—
1 in 1 trillion—that some people attribute it to divine intervention. Others conclude that perhaps the lottery is rigged. What
should we think about such events? What do they say about logic
and the laws of probability?

Just how unlikely is it that someone who has won a one-in-a-
million lottery will win it a second time? Well, let's suppose that
1,000 people have won such a lottery and that each of them tries
100 times to repeat the "miracle." That adds up to 100,000 chances
in a one-in-a-million lottery—or 1 in 10—that *someone* will repeat.
Not only is it not a miracle, it's not even a rare event.

As with the outguessing randomness trap, the surprised-by-
surprises trap results from a failure or an unwillingness to give reality its sometimes surprising due. Many people think themselves
truly anointed or gifted because they've won a succession of bets
(or made a series of very successful investments). But we should
not be impressed by these seemingly dramatic occurrences. Just
by chance, someone will be lucky. The chance that it will be *you* in
particular may be minuscule, but the chance that it will be *someone* in some context may not be all that small. Some wealthy
people out there may not be winners because of their business
acumen but because of sheer luck. But take heart: some unfortu-
nates may not be losers because of their stupidity or ineptness—
they may just be the unlucky ones.

When it comes to coincidence, people just don't think very
clearly. They can't accept the indifference of randomness. They

feel that they, personally, must have some special importance in and impact on the great impersonal universe. Believing, in effect, in divine or supernatural intervention, they become mystical in their own reasoning and suspicious of the probabilistic reasoning of others.

**What can you do about it?**   When a seemingly rare event occurs, don't be so surprised that you forsake logic and the laws of probability and believe instead that all rare events are preordained. Usually a good explanation can be found. Remember the following points:

- The world presents many potential surprises; you're bound to experience some of them.
- An enormous probabilistic gulf exists between an event's occurring when it has been flagged ahead of time—"I will meet my future wife by chance on the next subway train"—and when it has been identified later as interesting or significant—"I happened to meet my future wife on the subway two years ago."
- Some events that appear rare really aren't. What's the probability, for example, that you'll find a pair of people with the same birthday (day and month) out of 24 randomly chosen people? The answer is more than 50 percent!

## Forewarned Is Forearmed

Our brains are always at work—sometimes, unfortunately, in ways that hinder rather than help us. At every stage of the decision-making process, misperceptions, biases, and other tricks of the mind can distort the choices we make. Highly complex and highly important decisions are the most prone to distortion because they tend to involve the most assumptions and the most estimates. The higher the stakes, the higher the risks.

We're particularly vulnerable to traps involving uncertainty because most of us aren't naturally very good at judging chances. We *are* adept at judging time, distance, weight, and volume. That's because we're constantly making judgments about these variables and getting quick feedback about their accuracy. Through daily practice, our minds become finely calibrated. Judging uncertainty, however, is a different matter. Though we often make forecasts about uncertain events, we rarely get clear feedback about our accuracy.

If you assess, for example, that an event has a 40 percent chance of occurring and a different one occurs, you can't tell whether you were right or wrong. The only way to gauge your accuracy would be to keep track of many similar judgments to see if, after the fact, the events you thought had a 40 percent chance of occurring actually did occur 40 percent of the time. That would require a great deal of data, carefully tracked over a long period of time. Weather forecasters and bookmakers have incentives to maintain such records, but the rest of us don't. As a result, we never calibrate our brains for judging probabilities.

The best protection against all psychological traps is awareness. Forewarned is forearmed. Even if you can't eradicate the distortions ingrained in the way your mind works, you can build tests and disciplines into your decision-making process that can uncover and counter errors in thinking before they become errors in judgment.

Taking action to understand and avoid psychological traps has an added benefit: it will increase your confidence in the choices you make.

## Notes

Many of the specific examples in this chapter were first published in the scientific literature. The clarity/distance example (page 186) is from Amos Tversky and Daniel Kahneman, "Judgment Under Uncertainty: Heuristics and Biases," *Science* 185 (27 September 1974): 1124–1131. The mug/chocolate bar example (page 190) is from J. L. Knetsch, "The Endowment Effect and Evidence of Nonreversible Indifference Curves," *American Economic Review* 79 (1989):1277–1284. The death penalty example (page 195) is from C. G. Lord, L. Ross, and M. R. Lepper, "Biased Assimilation and Attitude Polarization: The Effects of Prior Series on Subsequently Considered Evidence," *Journal of Personality and Social Psychology* 37 (1979):2098–2109. The Pennsylvania/New Jersey insurance example (page 197) is from E. J. Johnson, J. Hershey, J. Meszaros, and H. Kunreuther, "Framing, Probability Distortions, and Insurance Decisions," *Journal of Risk and Uncertainty* 7 (1993): 35–51. The classic framing study (pages 197–198) is in Amos Tversky and Daniel Kahneman, "The Framing of Decisions and the Psychology of Choice," *Science* 211 (30 January 1981):453–458. The airline safety statistic (page 203) is from Arnold Barnett and Mary K. Higgins, "Airline Safety: The Last Decade," *Management Science* 35 (January 1989):1–22. The recalling of names example (pages 203–204) is from Amos Tversky and Daniel Kahneman, "Judgment Under Uncertainty: Heuristics and Biases," *Science* 185 (27 September 1974):1124–1131. The salesman/librarian example (pages 204–205) is from Daniel Kahneman and Richard Thaler as quoted in *Money*, June 1990, p. 87. Readers will find other interesting examples and traps described in these articles and in J. Edward Russo and Paul J. H. Schoemaker, *Decision Traps: The Ten Barriers to Brilliant Decision-Making and How to Overcome Them* (New York: Simon & Schuster, 1989), and Max Bazerman, *Judgment in Managerial Decision Making* (New York: John Wiley & Sons, 4th edition, 1998).

# CHAPTER 11

# The Wise Decision Maker

By NOW IT SHOULD BE CLEAR that the art of good decision making lies in systematic thinking. A systematic approach helps you to

- Address the right decision problem.
- Clarify your real objectives.
- Develop a range of creative alternatives.
- Understand the consequences of your decision.
- Make appropriate tradeoffs among conflicting objectives.
- Deal sensibly with uncertainties.
- Take account of your risk-taking attitude.
- Plan ahead for decisions linked over time.

It should also be clear that the concepts underlying a systematic approach are really rather simple. It may take a bit more time and effort to articulate your objectives carefully or to expand your set of alternatives, but the thought process itself is straightforward. In fact, the extra effort may not really be extra at all—it will often save you from endless wheel-spinning. And, most important, it will lead you to a better decision.

But making a smart decision is one thing. Becoming a *smart decision maker* is another. In this, our final chapter, we step back from the elements of a good decision-making approach to look at the ten core practices of the successful decision maker. We move from the process to the person. By mastering these practices, and applying them consistently, you will be well on your way to a lifetime of smart choices.

## Get Started

Procrastination is the bane of good decision making. Whatever the reason for putting off a decision—the problem seems hopelessly complex, deciding will be a lot of work, unpleasant emotions may arise—the need to decide won't go away.

Deciding by default, by *not* deciding, almost always yields unsatisfactory results, if only because you spend time wondering if you could have done better. So *get started*. The sooner you start, the more likely it is that you'll give your decision adequate thought and find adequate information, rather than being forced to decide in partial ignorance under pressure from the clock. Given time, too, your subconscious will aid your decision process, mulling over the problem and prompting solutions even as you attend to other things.

For a relatively painless jump-start, try answering the ten diagnostic questions listed on page 217. These will show you what you know and what you need to know to make a smart choice.

---

### Getting Started: Ten Diagnostic Questions

1. *What's my decision problem?* What, broadly, do I have to decide? What specific decisions do I have to make as a part of the broad decision?
2. *What are my fundamental objectives?* Have I asked "Why" enough times to get to my bedrock wants and needs?
3. *What are my alternatives?* Can I think of more good ones?
4. *What are the consequences of each alternative in terms of the achievement of each of my objectives?* Can any alternatives be safely eliminated?
5. *What are the tradeoffs among my more important objectives?* Where do conflicting objectives concern me the most?
6. *Do any uncertainties pose serious problems?* If so, which ones? How do they impact consequences?
7. *How much risk am I willing to take?* How good and how bad are the various possible consequences? What are ways of reducing my risk?
8. *Have I thought ahead, planning out into the future?* Can I reduce my uncertainties by gathering information? What are the potential gains and the costs in time, money, and effort?
9. *Is the decision obvious or pretty clear at this point?* What reservations do I have about deciding now? In what ways could the decision be improved by a modest amount of added time and effort?
10. *What should I be working on?* If the decision isn't obvious, what do the critical issues appear to be? What facts and opinions would make my job easier?

---

Once you do get started, don't let yourself get bogged down. Some decision makers become obsessed with each particular element of the process. They won't consider alternatives until they have a polished set of objectives. They won't spin out consequences until all possible alternatives are in place. And so on. Without the perspective that comes from looking ahead, these people always waste time on aspects of the decision problem that later turn out to be relatively unimportant. They may spend needless hours refining their objectives, for example, when the real issue is uncertainty, and when they finally get to uncertainty, they have too little time to do it justice.

Avoid this problem by beginning with a fire-drill analysis. For a simple or routine decision, imagine that you have only a few minutes to make it; for a more important and complex decision, imagine that you have only a few hours. Quickly run through all the decision elements: problem, objectives, alternatives, consequences, tradeoffs, uncertainties, risk tolerance, and linkage. Analyze each quickly. Don't get hung up on details. Don't worry about doing things just right. Try for an overview of your decision problem. See how the pieces fit together. This rough sketch should enhance your understanding of your problem. Armed with a perspective on the whole, you can later go back to specific points, tying off loose ends. And, often, you'll be pleasantly surprised to find that the fire-drill analysis led to a clear decision that, with little or no additional analysis, solved your problem. In any case, you'll be off and running.

## Concentrate on What's Important

For most decisions, you'll know right away what you need to focus on—it will be whatever is bothering you about the decision. Usually, there will be only one or two crucial elements; seldom will you be confronted by three or more.

If what's important isn't obvious, ask yourself "What's blocking me from making this decision? Why can't I just decide now?" The answer will indicate where you need to focus your attention. It may be uncertainty ("I don't know if this company will survive") or your basic problem definition ("I don't even know why this problem came up"). Whatever it is, review the relevant chapter's suggestions and buckle down.

## Develop a Plan of Attack

Once you've scoped out the decision and focused your sights, you'll next want to plan an orderly approach to find a resolution to your decision problem. Do you need information? Clearer objectives? Better alternatives? Proceed systematically to fill in the gaps, and then review your understanding of your decision problem as a whole.

Remember, however, that the problem definition may change as you dig in, so be flexible. Reexamine your strategy at regular intervals, and also stop and reflect whenever you have an unexpected insight or a burst of progress. Ask these kinds of questions:

- Is my decision obvious now?
- If not, is it worth more effort, or should I just pick the best contender?
- What have I learned? How has my perception of the problem changed?
- What should I work on next?

Revise your plan and continue. Repeat this process as necessary until your decision is made. A plan enables you to attack your decision problem in a disciplined way. But, at the same time, flexibility and openness to information and new developments are essential. Always be willing to stop, reassess, and reformulate your plan. Keep asking, "What's bothering me? What's blocking me? Why can't I just decide now?"

## Chip Away at Complexity

Many problems seem hopelessly complex, no matter how you define them. You seem to be making little progress and you find yourself hoping you'll somehow just muddle through. The following techniques will help you cope with some seemingly impossible situations.

**Make decisions in layers.**   With a series of interrelated decisions, start with the broadest one first (what job to take in a new city), work down to the next level (what neighborhood to live in), then further down to a more detailed level (what apartment to rent). At each level, make sure you have a sense of the most promising alternatives in the next level down, as they might influence your current, higher-level choice. (In selecting a job, for example, keeping in mind the desirability and affordability of nearby residential neighborhoods might help you decide, but the actual choice of a neighborhood and apartment would follow the job selection.) Large corporations and the military use this technique, making strategic decisions first, tactical decisions second, and operational decisions last.

**Zoom out and zoom in.**     The zoom technique, which takes its name from the action of zoom lenses, is a variation on the decisions-in-layers approach. Zooming out corresponds to looking at the big picture (the higher-level, strategic decision); zooming in corresponds to examining the details (the lower-level, tactical and operational decisions). With zooming, however, you don't make decisions at any level until you've considered decisions at each level several times. You start zoomed out and tentatively make the high-level decision, then you zoom in and consider how you would make several lower-level decisions that depend on the higher-level decision. Having done that, you zoom back out and reconsider the higher-level decision, armed with the perspective of having seen its implications at the lower level. You may zoom in and out several times before settling on the higher-level decision. Considering the impact on lower-level decisions serves as a reality check on the higher-level one before you make it.

**Compare consistent decision bundles.**     Certain choices naturally go together—they constitute consistent bundles. Suppose, for example, that you're a recent college graduate considering two job offers. If you take the engineering job in Los Angeles, you'll probably live in Westwood and study graduate-level engineering part-time at nearby UCLA. If, on the other hand, you take the product management job in San Francisco, you'll probably live in Berkeley and pursue graduate business courses part-time at U.C. Berkeley. In each case, having established a consistent set of choices encompassing job, where to live, and graduate work, you can compare the entire bundles.

**Pick the appropriate level of detail.** Match the level of detail in your analysis to the breadth of your problem definition; the broader the definition, the less detailed the analysis needs to be. Time after time, we see people greatly expand the breadth of a problem definition, maintain a high level of detail, and then complain about complexity. William James, the American philosopher, noted the phenomenon: "The art of being wise is knowing what to overlook." You must find, by trial and error, advice, or experience, the level of detail that works for the decision problem at hand.

## Get Unstuck

Many times in a decision-making process you may find yourself stuck, unable to make any forward progress. Sometimes you can't get started. Sometimes a seemingly insurmountable obstacle looms in your analysis of a key element. And sometimes, despite yards of analysis, you just can't make up your mind.

Our advice: find someone to talk to about your decision problem—let your mouth start your mind. Once you get talking, you'll see connections you never saw before. All the better if you prepare for the session by jotting down notes beforehand. Making notes will jog your mind; even if your helper backs out and you never meet, you will have advanced your thinking. Often we find that our consulting clients benefit more from preparing to meet with us and from the self-generated insights that result from explaining their problem than from any direct advice.

A good way to get unstuck is to imagine that you have to advise someone else who has a problem identical to yours. Consider

Keith's problem. Tormented by indecision, this 16-year-old world-class swimmer must decide whether to leave home for six months of training with other Olympic aspirants or to continue training at home with his excellent high school coach. Keith is a virtual cinch to make the U.S. Olympic team, and he wants the gold. But he is also loyal to his present coach and would miss his family and girlfriend if he went away. If he decides to go, he'll feel guilty; if he stays and wins only a bronze, he worries that he'll regret not having taken his best shot at the big prize. When he discusses his problem with us, we ask him, "If you had to give advice to someone else in exactly this same situation, what would you say?" He responds without hesitation: "Train with the best; leave home if you have to." And that's just what he did.

Another way out: if you face an obstacle to making a decision, consider what you would do if the obstacle disappeared. If money is the problem, for example, imagine that you have all you'll ever need. In many cases, you'll find that you'd do pretty much the same thing, obstacle or no. If you solve your decision problem by disregarding the obstacle, you can go back and figure out how to remove it.

## Know When to Quit

Analysis can continue forever, but you can't. Eventually, you'll have to decide. You therefore need to balance deliberation with speed. Obsessing over your decision takes a toll in time and psychological energy, but a hasty decision, rushed to avoid emotional stress or hard mental work, is usually a poor decision.

How do you know when enough is enough? You balance the

cost of putting in the extra effort against the benefit of *possibly* coming up with a better choice. These questions will help you decide:

- Do you feel you have a reasonable grasp of your decision problem?
- Have you already thoughtfully covered each element in the decision-making process relevant to your decision?
- Would you be satisfied if you chose one of the existing alternatives?
- Could the best alternatives disappear if you wait much longer?
- Is it unlikely that you could devise a new, better alternative with additional time for thought?
- Would a perfect solution be only slightly better than your current best alternative?
- Will taking more time for this decision seriously detract from your other important activities and decisions?

Clearly, if all or almost all your answers to these questions are "yes," you should quit analyzing and decide.

Sometimes you have to consciously protect yourself against overdoing it. "Analysis paralysis" manifests itself as an insatiable appetite for more and more information in an often-futile attempt to find a consideration that will clinch the decision one way or another or to uncover a perfect alternative. Seldom does a perfect solution exist, yet too may people endlessly (and unrealistically) pursue one. Often, the imagined need for more analysis becomes an excuse for procrastination, for avoiding a decision, because deciding will require accepting some bad along with the good.

## Use Your Advisors Wisely

To make a decision beyond your sphere of expertise, you'll often need to seek advice from others. These advisors, or experts, might include your doctor, lawyer, or accountant, to mention a few. Unfortunately, most people simply ask their advisor, "What should I do?" Then they follow the advice, even if they have a nagging discomfort about doing so.

Why the discomfort? If you ask your experts to decide for you, rather than help you to decide, your choices are unlikely to fully reflect your objectives, tradeoffs, and risk tolerance. If you want advice on what to decide, make sure you communicate your objectives, tradeoffs, and risk tolerance along with your perception of the problem. Better yet, decide for yourself after soliciting and incorporating their input on problem definition, alternatives, consequences, and uncertainties.

Use advisors for what they're good at—providing information about what is or what might be. Use your own judgment about what you know much better than they can—namely, your values and objectives. Then combine it all yourself and decide. After all, it's your choice.

## Establish Basic Decision-Making Principles

Minor, routine decisions rarely warrant a full-blown analysis. But although they may be relatively inconsequential as individual decisions, the sum of all of them can be very consequential. What you choose to have for dinner tonight is relatively inconsequential, but what you choose to eat over time adds up to determine your overall nutrition.

So, although you don't want to spend time pondering these decisions individually—whether they be personal or work-related—you will gain by making thoughtful decisions about the principles on which you make everyday choices. That way, when you decide routinely—almost on automatic pilot—your autopilot will have some policies (like eating well-balanced meals) built in that reflect your long-range values. In addition, your routine choices will be easier to make and require less effort if they are guided by these principles.

## Tune Up Your Decision-Making Style

Over time, you develop a decision-making style: a set of habits that governs your decision making. Of course, you'd like your style to be as effective and efficient as possible, and you'll want to keep working to improve it. The best way to do this is to periodically review your performance on several of your recent decisions. To facilitate the review and the resulting learning, write down the basis and logic for each of your important decisions at the time you make them. Use these notes in your evaluation. Look for patterns. What does your behavior tell you about your style? For instance,

- Are your alternatives imaginative enough?
- Do you spend too much time on less important issues?
- Do you tend to gravitate toward choices that, after the fact, seem too conservative?

- Do you feel that you are in control of your decision making, or do decisions just happen to you?

Having done a review, are you happy with your style? Does it help or hinder you in achieving what you want? What, if anything, would you change? What should you work on?

You can do the reviews by yourself, but using a partner can often provide greater insight. Ask a family member, friend, or colleague to help you evaluate some decisions with which they may be familiar. Offer to reciprocate. The benefits to each of you will be manifold: in addition to gaining an outside perspective on your decision-making techniques, you will benefit from seeing another's approach and from doing some coaching.

But be careful not to judge your or your partner's decision making solely by the desirability of the consequences. Remember, you must distinguish between smart choices and good consequences. It's following a sound process that matters; smart choices are more likely to lead to good consequences, but you'll get some bad ones, too.

It's fair to ask, however, whether you fully anticipated the possible consequences of your decisions. Did outcomes occur that you never even thought of when you made your decision? You can't think of everything, but if you find too many situations where you've completely missed something important, you aren't being sufficiently thorough in defining your problem and in anticipating consequences.

How can you improve? Practice. All skills require practice.

## Take Charge of Your Decision Making

Who should make your decisions? You should. So who should be choosing the decision problems that you face? Once again, *you*—whenever possible. We urge you to take the initiative in your decision making rather than wait for decision situations to come to you.

Decision problems are often dropped onto your shoulders by others (competitors, bosses, family) or by circumstances (mother nature, accidents, financial markets). Life would obviously be better if many such problems disappeared. No parent, after all, wants to see a bright child doing poorly in school, no manager wants to see a good product losing market share to an upstart competitor, and no homeowner wants to see a sound house damaged by strong winds. The decision problems arising from these situations are not appealing.

To the extent possible, therefore, it is better to proactively create your own decision problems. Decision problems created by you are decision opportunities, not problems. We all have a fundamental interest in being healthy, for example. This interest suggests numerous decision opportunities: How can one best remain or become fit? How should one learn to eat responsibly? How can one reduce driving risks?

You needn't address these questions, but you have the opportunity to do so. Take an opportunity and use the ideas in this book to appraise, decide, and act. If you don't take these opportunities, you lessen your chances of remaining in good health. The decision problems that you subsequently face will be less appealing: Where should one go for triple bypass surgery? How does one get around if one can no longer drive?

The spark for identifying decision opportunities is clarifying something that you want. There is a way to be systematic about this. It's called *value-focused thinking* because it begins with your values, what you hold to be of worth, useful, and desirable. Begin by sitting down and defining a high-level set of objectives—your values—specifying what you want from life or from some aspect of it, such as your career, marriage, family, hobbies, or whatever. For at-work decision making, define values for your organization or your part of it.

Then use these values to seek out and create decision opportunities. For the value "have more leisure time," for example, determine how best to fulfill it. By taking the initiative, you will increase your control over your future by increasing your options.

One particularly good way to take charge is to view your life as a sequential decision problem—to think ahead. Consider Dianne Morris, a bright college junior who is considering becoming a doctor. "I'm not *sure* I want to be a doctor. I just *think* I want to be a doctor."

"How about a biologist or psychologist?"

"Well, maybe. I know I don't want to be an entrepreneur, or a musician, or an astronaut."

The truth is that Dianne, like many college students, has unclear ambitions that will change with life's experiences. Still, she knows that she wants to be an independent woman, earning a wage that will enable her to have interesting and rewarding experiences; she knows, or thinks she knows, that she wants to help people. She knows she has taken and likes tough science courses. The fact is that she knows a lot about herself, though there's still a lot she doesn't know.

Without any coaching, Dianne is already looking steps ahead.

At an early age she knew that if she wanted to be a doctor she'd have to go to college and therefore had to get good grades in high school. She knew that she had better study math because she would need that to take science courses. She read about some famous doctors because she wanted an idea of what their lives were like. She worked in a lab, not only to get experience but to assess whether lab work should be part of her future career. She is already a systematic, qualitative thinker—looking ahead, learning along the way, adapting, testing, making commitments, backing off, exploring new byways, gathering information to learn what new information to gather.

Should Dianne practice more formalized decision making at this point? Would she be helped by assessing probabilities for the uncertainties she faces? Should she be recording her desirability scores for different paths down her decision tree of life? No! A resounding no! We do think, however, that Dianne would profit, as we all might, from being a little more conscious of the process and a little more systematic in thinking through it. Periodically, she may wish to take stock.

- She might reexamine her interests. What does she want, really want, when she grows up?
- She might clarify some of her long-range aspirations: Does she want both a family and a career?
- She should identify and clarify some of the key uncertainties that, once better known, would help her better choose a wise direction to pursue.
- She might want to think about gathering information that could help point her in appropriate directions—information gathered from asking friends, from reading books, from electing courses, from seeking jobs, from participat-

ing in extracurricular activities, from joining clubs, from
traveling, from volunteering to help others. She should try
to seek information efficiently. Some information may be
relevant to lots of specific uncertainties. Some types of information may be less costly than others to acquire.

- She should set some intermediate goals. Learning how to
write well and enhancing her computer skills are option
wideners that would provide flexibility for a wide range of
intellectual pursuits. Developing interpersonal skills would
stand her in good stead whether she became a doctor, a
psychologist, a social worker, or something else entirely.

- She should put herself in a position so that, when surprises
come, they will be more likely to enhance the quality of her
future choices.

- She should further develop skill at making smart choices.

Living is a balancing act between errors of two kinds: Dianne
could be so worried about the future that she doesn't enjoy the
present, or she could be so involved in the present that she
doesn't accumulate skills and intellectual capital for the future.
Thinking about this, she should proactively guide herself to her
own best balance.

## What's in It for You?

You have a lot to gain by using the ideas in this book to guide your
decision making. To get the full benefit, though, you have to
work at it. Try the PrOACT approach on several of your decisions.
Begin with important decisions, but not your most critical life decisions. It may seem awkward or cumbersome at first, like changing your tennis stroke. But soon you'll be at ease. You'll feel as if

this is how you wanted to think about decisions all along. The approach offers you a more systematic way to do what you do naturally every day.

As you come to use the method routinely, you will find that the benefits come relatively easily. You will discover that

- Most tough decision problems have one, or maybe two, difficult elements.
- Many of your tough decisions aren't as hard as they look. By being systematic and focusing on the hard parts, you can resolve them comfortably.
- Describing the problem, clarifying objectives, and coming up with good alternatives form the foundation of good decisions. In well over half of all decisions, a good job on these three elements will lead quickly to a good decision.
- Identifying and eliminating poor alternatives almost always provides a big benefit, especially when they weren't obviously inferior at the outset. This discipline keeps you from making a foolish choice, ensures a good choice when differences among the remaining alternatives are small, and often greatly simplifies the decision.
- When there is uncertainty, you can't guarantee that good consequences will result when you've made a smart choice. But over time, luck favors people who follow good decision-making procedures.

Most important, always remember: the only way to exert control over your life is through your decision making. The rest just happens to you. Be proactive, take charge of your decision making, strive to make good decisions and to develop good decision-making habits. You'll be rewarded with a fuller, more satisfying life.

# A Roadmap to
# Smart Choices

# About the Authors

**Dr. John S. Hammond** is a management consultant based in Lincoln, Massachusetts, known for helping his clients make tough choices. He blends the rigors of sound theory with extensive practical experience from four decades in industry, academia, and consulting. Dr. Hammond has worked in the computer division of NCR; taught at the Harvard Business School and at MIT's Sloan School of Management; and consulted for the American Stock Exchange, Bank of America, CIGNA, DuPont, Estée Lauder, General Electric, IBM, the United Nations, the World Bank, and scores of other organizations. He is the coauthor of *Strategic Market Planning* and a coauthor of *Management Decision Sciences*. He also wrote or supervised more than 100 Harvard case studies. Dr. Hammond's articles have appeared in the *Harvard Business Review*, the *Sloan Management Review*, the *Journal of Finance*, *Management Science*, and other journals.

**Dr. Ralph L. Keeney** is a professor at the University of Southern California in the Marshall School of Business and the School of Engineering and affiliated with the Center for Telecommunications Management. He is especially known for his work on making difficult tradeoffs. He also has a private consulting practice, based in San Francisco, where his clients include American Express, British Columbia Hydro, the Electric Power Research Institute, Kaiser Permanente, Pacific Gas and Electric, Seagate, and the U.S. Department of Energy. Dr. Keeney is the author of *Value-Focused Thinking: A Path to Creative Decisionmaking* and coauthor of *Decisions with Multiple Objectives,* winner of the 1976 Lanchester Prize. He was the founder and, for seven years, the leader of the decision and risk analysis group of a major geotechnical and environmental consulting firm. Dr. Keeney was previously a professor at MIT and was elected to the National Academy of Engineering.

**Dr. Howard Raiffa** is a pioneer in the development of decision analysis, negotiation analysis, and the theory of games. He has taught the art and science of decision making at Harvard University for the past four decades. Throughout that time, half of his professorial appointment has been at the Harvard Business School, and half has been distributed among the Division of Engineering and Applied Sciences, the Economics Department, the Kennedy School of Government, the Law School, the School of Public Health, and the Statistics Department. Dr. Raiffa has supervised nearly 100 doctoral dissertations. His writings, and his students, have influenced the teaching and practice of decision making in universities throughout the world. Among his most influential authored and coauthored books are *Games and Decisions, Decision Analysis, Decisions with Multiple Objectives,* and *The Art and Science of Negotiation.* Professor Raiffa helped negotiate the establishment of the International Institute for Applied Systems Analysis (IIASA), an international think tank in Vienna, and served as its first director. In the 1970s, its aim was to bridge the political divide between East and West through applied science; in the 1990s, its mission has become to study global environment problems.